VISIONS OF CYCLING

GRAHAM WATSON

VISIONS OF CYCLING

SBL SPRINGFIELD BOOKS LIMITED

Published by Springfield Books Limited,
Norman Road, Denby Dale, Huddersfield
HD8 8TH, West Yorkshire, England

First edition 1989

British Library Cataloguing in Publication Data
Watson, Graham *1956 Mar. 18 –*
    Visions of Cycling.
    1. Bicycles. Racing
    I. Title
    796.6'2

ISBN 0 947655 50 6

Design: Douglas Martin Associates
Typesetting: Armitage Typo/Graphics Ltd, Huddersfield
Printed and bound in Hong Kong by Colorcraft Ltd

Frontispiece: *The glacier of la Lauzière towering over Herrera
and Parra on the Col de la Madeleine, 1988*

CONTENTS

Allan Peiper in action in a time trial. Giro d'Italia, 1986

FOREWORD

by Allan Peiper

In the last ten years professional cycling has changed dramatically, from a three-nation European sport to a growing worldwide business. France, Belgium and Italy have enjoyed their cycling pre-eminence since its beginnings a hundred years ago, and made no serious attempts to share this glorious sport with the rest of the world. Since the mid-1970s, however, there has been a fantastic increase in the numbers of English-speaking, Scandinavian and South American riders. This may not be the only reason why cycling has achieved such widespread popularity, but it has helped to break down the barriers that kept cycling locked inside Europe. Greg LeMond winning the Tour de France in 1986 brought home cycling to America; Phil Anderson's courage made him a hero all over Europe, and now every Australian knows what the Tour de France is about; Luis Herrera became the 'Emperor of Colombia' with his 1987 Tour of Spain – a farmer's son, Herrera gave a glimmer of hope to the poverty-stricken peasants of his country.

But the biggest change in the cycling world has been brought about by Sean Kelly and Stephen Roche. In 1987 Roche re-wrote the record books by winning the Giro d'Italia, Tour de France and World Championships all in one year. Kelly, though he has never won the Tour or a World Championship, has been the undisputed champion of the sport for the last ten years, living up to his nickname of 'King Kelly'.

The exploits of these new heroes have been chronicled by a new breed of journalists and photographers; their success has been paralleled by the rise in numbers of English-speaking pressmen making the sport accessible to a new public. Fitting into such a European sport as cycling has not been easy for them: the language barrier has had to be overcome, and many of them have had to learn about the sport from the ground up. Only by winning the respect of their European counterparts have they achieved the working conditions necessary for the practice of their craft.

One of these men is Graham Watson. It must have been hard enough to gain admittance to the ranks of the European press, but the regard in which he is also held by the race organisers, motorbike drivers and fellow-photographers reflects the reputation he has earned over the last ten or twelve years. He has become my close friend, but most of all a man I respect because of his tireless working ability, which stems from his deep love of cycling.

The work of photographers often goes unacknowledged, save for a cursory by-line in magazines and newspapers: not for them the applause of the fans or the trophy that we riders might receive. They might not suffer the same, but the photographers are subjected to the same dangers and discomforts as we are, recording every turn of our pedals, our smiling faces when we win and – with great enthusiasm! – our grimaces when we fall.

Paralleling the rise of the new generation of cyclists, so Graham's work has gone from strength to strength: he is now at the top of his profession, and his pictures are in demand all over the world. His insight into cycling and cyclists astounds me. A man who always has the welfare of the riders in the forefront of his mind, whether racing or not, Graham is a credit to his profession.

INTRODUCTION

In *Visions of Cycling* I have set out to show the attractions of cycle racing through the eyes of a photographer, because a photographer can see the sport in a uniquely unshackled way. Editorial needs, of course, have to be met: the race-winning break, the winner on the finish line, the obligatory podium shot: but beyond that he is free to see the race – and, from the back of a motorbike, seeing so much more, and sharing so much closer a relationship with the riders, than a journalist ever can – his own way. My creative freedom is limited only by my own talent and ingenuity.

My fascination with this still unspoilt and underestimated sport is all-embracing. I thrill at the sight of a speeding bunch in any situation and any land, rain or shine, bleak or colourful; I marvel at their courage; glory in their victories; hurt when they crash. The physical impact of these superb athletes is hard to over-state: glistening muscles bulging and contracting to a punishing, yet hypnotic, pedalling rhythm, effort and determination etched into every strained line of their faces. And the magnificent backdrop to their heroic performances: the landscapes through which the road races pass. What other sport takes its fans out on the open road, on windswept plains, up and down mountain passes, through snow and rain, blistering heat and dust, all over the world? And yet cycle racing manages to keep, by virtue of the hardly-varying racing season, its sense of coherence: over the months of a season, as each race rolls into another, it is easy to forget who won what and how, but the landscapes act like a beacon, guiding my thoughts forward or back to each event. The landscape cannot change, and because the routes of many of the great races have remained unchanged for decades, each one keeps its character from year to year, easily distinguished from the rest of the season but very much part of it.

My visions of cycling reflect the growth of interest in the sport in the English-speaking nations. When I first showed a photographic interest in cycling, riders like Sean Kelly, Paul Sherwen, Phil Anderson and Greg LeMond had barely made an impact on what was then considered a purely continental sport. Since then, an ever-increasing number of cyclists from countries outside mainland Europe have joined the teams, some of them finding success in a big way. My career has flourished alongside theirs: with their success has come a ready market for my work.

It's very pleasant having 'friends in the peloton', and it can be a valuable source of information, but for a photographer it can also be a drawback: sharing a background, or at least a language, with a cyclist eliminates some of the mystery which for me is one of the main attractions. Capturing the expressions of riders who remain aloof – and therefore mysterious – is a challenge: Bernard Hinault, Francesco Moser, Pedro Delgado, Laurent Fignon, Claude Criquielion . . .

As an 'interloper' into a sport whose roots are firmly entrenched in mainland Europe, it would have been tough to gain acceptance without the help and support of more people than I could ever mention here. The bulk of my career experiences have been shared with John Wilcockson, whom I first met in 1981 at the world championships in Czechoslovakia; meeting by chance, we discovered that at home we lived less than three miles apart! Our working relationship developed, and I had the privilege of working with John on several magazines, including *Cyclist Monthly, Winning* and *Inside Cycling.* Those magazines allowed us to indulge our mutual passion for the sport, a passion which has opened many doors for us. Of all the adventures we've shared, one stands out from all the rest.

In 1987, on the day Stephen Roche deposed Roberto Visentini in the Giro d'Italia, John and I managed to sneak the back way into Roche's hotel in Sappada – the front was sealed off against the angry crowds milling outside – and two minutes later found ourselves admitted to his room and sitting on the end of his bed. We talked until late into the night about the fight he had on his hands, with his own team and the seriously partisan Italian crowds, and left his room fired up with enthusiasm for his cause. Irish we were not, but his courage, and the enormity of what he had taken on, sent us off like two fellow-conspirators to ask Sean Yates if he would help Stephen in the difficult days ahead. At gone midnight, and outside the very door of Yates's room, our professional judgement reasserted itself: what on earth did we think we were doing . . .

Working closely with John also taught me the value of a mutually beneficial relationship between words and pictures. However incisive a description of a race, however dramatic a picture, they are almost always further illuminated by their visual or written counterpart. It is this relationship I have attempted to communicate in *Visions of Cycling;* without some explanation, a picture of Pedro Delgado climbing Guzet Neige, however dramatic or beautiful, remains just that – a picture. By adding an explanation of the thought and skill that went into getting that picture, I hope the vision will become more complete.

It was John who introduced me to Robin Magowan in 1983 at the Omloop Het Volk in Belgium. Less than a week later Robin and I were sharing a new set of adventures on the circuit, and it was at Robin's instigation that we co-authored *Kings of the Road* in 1986. Robin's outlook on the sport is in complete contrast to John's, and yet they share a high place in my esteem. Other friends have motivated and supported me in a way that only true friends can. My work in the past five years has brought me close to two people in particular: Ann McQuaid and Louis 'Lucho' Viggio have a place deep in my affections, having shared some of my happier moments and, without knowing it, enabled me to shrug off some less-happy ones. It's great knowing you!

Motorbikes – and more particularly their drivers – play a large part in getting pictures. Their presence in the peloton is often misinterpreted, but is in fact dictated by the need to be there when something happens. And when something does happen, a good driver is essential. I'd like to pay tribute to all the drivers who have tolerated my frantic shouting and shoulder-thumping, particularly Patrice Diallo (France and Italy), Rene Tampère (Belgium) and Philippe Borguet and Jan Wouters (Tour de France): without you, it wouldn't be possible!

It is also fair to acknowledge some of my foreign colleagues, with whom I share so many experiences, and not a little rivalry – for it's the element of competition that has produced many of the working highlights recalled in *Visions of Cycling.* Amongst the following names are one or two people who have inspired me, by virtue of their own deep commitment, to take better pictures: Cor Vos from Holland, Aldo Tonnoir from Belgium, Italy's Sergio Penazzo, and from France, Georges Rakič, Denys Clement and Henri Besson. Henri is the doyen of cycling photographers, with more than twenty Tours de France to his credit, the first of which, in 1967, proved to be a tragic baptism – photographing the collapse and death of Tommy Simpson on Mont Ventoux. It was Besson's work in *Miroir-Sprint* and *Miroir du Cyclisme* which heightened the profile of cycling photography and drew many of us younger photographers into the sport.

Life as a professional cycling photographer is like no other: endless travelling, the mixture of cultures, meeting and making new friends, in some of the world's most picturesque and historic locations; as well as working in, and with, the peloton. It is a privileged profession, and one that is only possible thanks to the presence of so many – and such photogenic – cyclists. It is to this rare breed of men that *Visions of Cycling* is dedicated.

Pedro Delgado approaching Gazet Neige, Tour de France, 1988. The image of man versus nature — of cyclist versus mountain — is a perpetual source of inspiration. But pictures like this don't just happen — they are the result of technical and compositional skill as well as patience and cool thinking. All these factors come together as the photographer's 'feel' for his chosen sport takes over, capturing his memorable shot, arguably the ultimate image of cycling . . .

It's not only cyclists who crash! I came a cropper in the 1988 Paris-Nice when my driver Patrice (with his back to the camera) hit a patch of oil and rammed the doctor's car. All the other drivers rushed to help us, and we managed to pull the bike from under the car and drive on, but not before Bernard Charlet of France-Soir *had recorded the scene for posterity!*

A RACE WITHIN A RACE

The room was crammed to capacity, perhaps as many as seventy men gathering for the meeting in the sports centre at l'Alpe d'Huez on the evening of 14 July 1988. Just four hours earlier, the same men had been involved in what looked like a serious breach of conduct as the twelfth stage of the Tour de France reached its conclusion on the roads leading to this famous ski-station.

The trouble was that a series of attacks by Fabio Parra of Colombia had been frustrated by an armada of press motorbikes, only for Holland's Steven Rooks to slip away in the ensuing confusion and win the prestigious stage. Altogether it was a serious affair, and from the faces of the officials filing into the room, you would have guessed some of us at least were going to get our marching orders. It was race director Xavier Louy who spoke first, to explain how the 'inquest' would be held, but the first words he spoke were not of anger or reprimand but of surprise: 'Well,' he began, visibly taken aback by the size of the assembled mass, 'I'm sure now we can all see why today's problems happened.'

It was simpler to explain what happened than to prevent it happening again. For the entire 13 km climb of 'the Alpe' the leading duo, Delgado and Rooks, had been chased by Parra and Theunisse. As the leaders tired towards the end of the stage so their chasers got closer: so close, in fact, that for the first time in the Tour's many visits to the Alpe a group of riders came together in the closing minutes, just as thousands of spectators narrowed the road. In front of the riders were slowly moving officials' cars, guests' cars, in fact all kinds of cars. Around the riders, the world's massive media entourage, mounted on thirty-odd motorbikes. The result was inevitable – the road was blocked. Rooks had been quick to take advantage of this confusion, jumping into the jam of motorbikes as they tried to accelerate away from the mess. Live television had shown three successive attacks by Parra frustrated by the close

proximity of so many motorbikes. Hence the hastily-organised meeting, to which all the motorbike drivers and photographers had been summoned.

Exactly twelve months previously a one-day strike had been successfully staged by the photographers in protest at their cavalier treatment at the hands of the organisers. Now, on the same mountain, the organisers were asking us to help them out, to try and solve the problems caused by the ever-increasing demands of the world's media, problems that we ourselves encounter on an almost daily basis, not just on the Tour but throughout the whole season. Unfortunately, however good the relationship between the riders and the photographers, there is a very fine line to tread (and that at high speed) between great shots and consideration, and occasionally there is bound to be a conflict between these two demands.

Cycle racing can be photographed in two main ways; from the side of the road, using a good map and a fast car; and by joining the race on a motorbike. The diversion method is perfectly adequate for the majority of photographers who only need three or four good shots from each race. The motorbike is essential for agency or newspaper photographers and Europe's leading cycle magazines, who all require in-depth coverage. It's also the most sought-after means of transport, so only a select few succeed in following races this way.

We are a mixed bunch; mainly French and Belgian with one Englishman and the odd Dutch or Italian, but drawn together in our common cause – showing the world our sport through the medium of photography. In many respects our lives are not dissimilar to those of the riders themselves, a nomadic existence on the nine-month-long trek round the great races of Europe. We too have our rivalries and alliances, our successes and setbacks. But always, no matter how fierce the competition between ourselves, our collective strength

enables us to close ranks when our interests are threatened.

This unity derives mainly from our shared experience, particularly of the arduous conditions; before the major races like the Giro d'Italia and the Tour de France in June and July this very select group will have slipped and slithered over greasy cobblestones in the Belgian spring classics, choked in the dust of a dry Paris-Roubaix and then, barely a week later, been frozen to the marrow in a snow-stormed Liège-Bastogne-Liège. And as if the weather wasn't enough, there's an additional – and perhaps the greatest – problem: working the territory around the moving peloton.

This is where the motorbike photographer earns his identity. There are three formations, each one with greatly differing needs; service cars, which travel on the right of the road behind the race; press cars, which travel on the left of the road in front and behind; and press motorbikes, which occupy the coveted area immediately behind and to the left of the cyclists. Additionally, the race director and race doctor travel in separate cars immediately behind and to the right of the race, together with one or two sponsors' cars. It all makes for a congested area, but somehow a code of conduct, distilled from years of experience, attempts to ensure that the three groups respect each others' requirements as much as possible. And the motorbike photographers pay for their privilege: not for us the comfort of a snug, warm car. We work out there in the wind and rain, duelling with each other and the overtaking press cars, risking our necks whenever a team car comes up to service one of the riders.

Of course, the code of conduct involves a hierarchy. This hierarchy, or pecking order, is most in evidence in the Tour de France, where the sheer scale of the race demands that someone must be seen to be imposing discipline within the corps of motorbike photographers. If we have a 'patron', it is the French motorbike driver

from *L'Equipe,* Jacques Garcia. Whichever photographer he is driving for, Garcia carries a lot of clout with race organisers in Europe, thanks largely to the fact that *L'Equipe* is the most respected sports newspaper in the world. So it is only to be expected that most of us turn to Garcia to put a point across during a race. He's also arguably the best driver currently working the scene . . . and whilst the extent of his influence is not to everyone's taste, his authority does help to impose discipline and thus safeguard the riders.

Driving in a big race is a highly skilled, often dangerous job, and both driver and photographer have to function as one unit in order to work well and safely. For this reason, any newcomer with a less-than-capable driver is likely to see little of the real action, finding his access continually blocked by other drivers. Buying-in – literally – to the inner circle of drivers can be a good investment. Instead of wasting all your energy trying to direct the driver into position – and usually finding your way blocked by a solid wall of motorbikes – now, miraculously, a gap opens in that wall. Shooting from in front of the riders, your view of the race remains unobscured, whereas before another photographer's bike would somehow get itself between you and the riders so that he, not you, got the pictures that mattered. As a photographer's or driver's experience increases, so gradually does he become accepted and trusted by Garcia and the other top drivers.

To a newcomer all this can be very unnerving. When you venture out in a race on a motorbike, and later on, draw close to the action to shoot some pictures, you can feel critical eyes studying your every movement. And you'll know if you're not wanted there; a shout from the riders or a blast from an official's whistle are only a breath away. The official task of controlling press motorbikes falls to the race director and a commissaire, who may himself be aboard a motorbike. All bikes on the race must be fitted with a one-way VHF radio, or 'scanner', so that officials' instructions can be heard immediately. These radios are checked by the commissaire before each race and anyone without a radio – or whose radio doesn't work – is off the race. (Two-way radios are not allowed, as officials want their instructions carried out immediately and not debated over the airwaves.) You are given a printed cardboard disc or plaque which, fixed to the front of the motorbike, identifies your role in the event. Photographers must often wear numbered bibs so that an official can identify them personally on the race radio.

For the most part, photographers prefer to view the race from behind, especially at the beginning, when there is more likelihood of crashes or other incidents. But once the race reaches a decisive point – the 120-km mark in the Tour of Flanders, for instance – they move in front, staying sixty metres ahead of the race, or going on ahead to a particular point of interest, for example, the Koppenberg. Sometimes it's an impossibility to overtake a packed 200-strong bunch in full flight, and photographers can find themselves trapped amongst the riders if they time their move badly. Working ahead of the race requires a mixture of qualities from driver and photographer. Once the cameraman spots something he wants, a tap on the driver's shoulder sets the sequence in motion. The driver has to drop back to the riders, immediately adjusting his speed precisely to theirs – not an easy thing if the road is undulating or twisting – and all the time looking in his mirrors in case a rider jumps into the motorbike's slipstream. At the same time he has to anticipate the road ahead; the riders can go downhill and around corners quicker than a motorbike. Having got to the spot, and very aware of the other motorbikes in action around him, the photographer will fire away. He will already have decided on the type of picture he's after, selected his camera and lens combination and adjusted his exposure; he has between

Jacques ('the Boss') Garcia posing with Denys Clement before a stage of Tirreno-Adriatico

A typical photographer's view of the Tour de France: framed by television cameraman, Roche and Lejarreta climb l'Alpe d'Huez, 1987

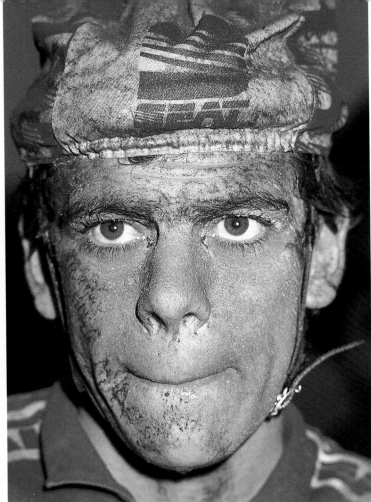

five and eight seconds to get his shots, no more — and often less, if the race is alive with attacks. Experience will tell the duo when to move away, but all the time the race director's voice will be coming over the radio instructing — sometimes begging — the driver to go away. It probably won't be the first time, either; one of the race director's biggest anxieties is to make sure that no press motorbike interferes with or 'makes' the racing.

Once a group or individual has established a decent lead — never less than thirty seconds — motorbikes are permitted to drop in behind, giving the photographer another view of what is perpetually a photogenic subject. Here, away from the tension that envelops a compact peloton, both driver and photographer can relax a little, sitting back to wait for an opportunity to present itself. Behind a breakaway group, the drivers adopt a more casual approach, operating a rota system

so that each photographer spends a minute or two immediately behind the rider or group before moving aside and letting someone else take his place. And if a photographer wants to go ahead and shoot from the front, he just instructs his driver, and having got the nod from the race director, overtakes to do his work, dropping back again when he's finished.

Naturally, once the pressure is on again — perhaps a steep hill (one of a photographer's favourite locations because of the strain on the riders' faces) is looming up — it's every man for himself as we jockey for the best position in front of and behind the riders. In theory it is possible for everybody to get a shot of the action on a climb of reasonable length, but in practice once three or four motorbikes are in position it is well nigh impossible to break through; it is a measure of a driver's skill to hog his piece of road for as long as possible and stop a rival photographer getting a shot. There can be

Van Vliet, Cabestany, Hinault and Herrera: studies in exhilaration, melancholy, geniality and hauteur respectively, captured with varying degrees of awareness on their part. Once on their bikes, they will cease to notice our existence as we work amidst the jostling, pulsing peloton

a moment in a big event — say, Hinault attacking alone in the final kilometres of the 1984 Tour of Lombardy — when twenty photographers want a picture. Not everyone can get *the* moment — it's all over in a few seconds. But a skilled driver/photographer combination will have foreseen any such moments and reacted before the race director and most of the other photographers have woken up to the situation. This is a skill where Jacques Garcia has no equals.

As befits its lofty status, the Tour de France brings together the finest, most reputable drivers. The inner circle of drivers is most in its element in this race, influencing the behaviour of all the press motorbikes. It is here too that you reap the benefits of respecting Garcia's leadership in other races. In a sport dominated by commercial interests television is supreme, and all

non-TV motorbikes are obliged to move aside whenever and wherever the cameramen decide they want to film. While this may be good for the organisers' bank balances, it is bad news for us photographers: that it doesn't make our job impossible is partly due to Garcia, who, by virtue of the regard in which he is held by the television drivers, makes sure that we all get a piece of the action. For although the Tour organisers try to see to it that all media people work in the best possible conditions, it is out there on the open road where the real battle is fought — usually in the first week of the race when each group of drivers sets out to impose its authority on the others.

Raul Alcala. Following the race on a motorbike enables the photographer to get close to the action. Here on l'Alpe d'Huez in 1987 I spot this Mexican cyclist wringing the sweat out of his jersey

A race within a race

Sharing the same road – and often the same traumas – as the riders makes the relationship between rider and photographer a special one, and one which both parties respect. There are many times, especially during a stage race, when pleasantries are exchanged, and it's not uncommon to see a rider handing a scrap of food to a photographer who has missed out on his breakfast! There are more practical advantages to this relationship; riders often ask for information on the approaching section of the race: 'How far to go?'; 'How far ahead is the break?'; 'What about that last climb?' are some of the questions asked, and from time to time, the photographer will act as a porter, relieving a rider of his unwanted spare jersey or racing cape, thus saving the rider from having to ride back to his team car and wasting valuable energy in the process.

Surprisingly, the riders claim that when the racing gets serious they scarcely notice our presence. At times this is hard to believe, given some of the situations we find ourselves in, caught in a big stack-up, or trapped in the middle of a descending bunch as our passing move is thwarted by an increase in the pace or a sudden narrowing of the road. Occasionally, a photographer's motorbike can cause pile-ups during a race: always regrettable, but sometimes unavoidable. Incidents like that, apart from the injuries they cause to the riders, reflect badly on our presence in the peloton. We rely heavily on the tolerance of the riders to do our jobs, in what is always a difficult and often a dangerous task. But, as the Australian rider Allan Peiper says, 'We know you've got a job to do as well as we have, so why should we object to you being there?'

A breakaway in the 1983 Omloop Het Volk closely attended by motorbike photographers

The colourful sight of the peloton in all its glory for the first time in the season. The 1988 Milan-San Remo, snaking along the Mediterranean coast

THE WORKING YEAR

For riders and press alike the racing season is long, beginning in early March with the Omloop Het Volk. Then Milan-San Remo marks the start of the prestigious spring classics, followed by the major Tours, and the season finally comes to an end in Italy eight months on with the Giro di Lombardia – everyone's sentimental favourite. Given Italy's aristocratic standing in cycling it is only fitting that her two international classics should act like bookends to the entire racing calendar, containing the kaleidoscope of images and memories of the season that stay in the mind long after the press reports and pictures have faded.

But before the season can begin properly, the committed photographer feels obliged to take in at least one of the training races that abound in the warmer countries of Europe at that time of the year. For the cyclists, these races are a vitally important preparation for the season, getting to know new team-mates as well as easing themselves back into a racing mood. The photographer too must acquaint himself with new faces and new team colours (it takes several races to adapt to familiar faces in unfamiliar colours) and generally brush up his reflexes for the coming one-day events. Failure to do adequate homework can prove costly later; in a one-day event you only get one chance at the best pictures, and when the riders are covered in mud, trying to pick out individuals is even more difficult. Even so, it can be mid-April before one is really tuned-in to the season.

We also take advantage of the more relaxed atmosphere of a warm-up race to chat at length with the riders, knowing too well that they won't give us another chance till after the Tour de France, when the pressures have eased. Only rarely does one get to know a rider well, but having a good rapport with as many of them as possible can reap benefits when it comes to taking their pictures. Since their contracts are directly related to their column inches, most riders are reasonably cooperative!

Belgium's Omloop Het Volk, although not officially a classic, is the traditional opening battle, held always on the first Saturday in March. Not much in the always cold, usually wet conditions to inspire the photographer, the main characteristic of this event is that it renews the rivalries of the Dutch and Belgian riders who, competing on home soil, habitually dominate the racing. It is rare indeed to catch an outstanding shot here: apart from the slippery ascent of the Geraardsbergen cobbles and the equally testing bash along the Paddiestraat, it's the racing shots – bleakly attractive as they are – that we fall back on. It's not surprising that the Het Volk, and to a lesser extent the ensuing Paris-Nice, are for this photographer merely a warm-up for the first highlight of my working year – Milan-San Remo.

Milan-San Remo

For the few of us who have covered Spanish, Belgian and French races already that season, the powerful Italian ambience of Milan in mid-March comes as a culture shock. And since few Italian cyclists will have been seen abroad before Milan-San Remo, the photographer hasn't had a chance to familiarise himself with the new Italian teams and colours; such is the status of Italian cycling that proper preparation is essential. Fortunately, recent changes in the racing calendar have meant that it is possible to work the last five days of Paris-Nice before dashing off to the far side of Italy to catch the last three days of Tirreno-Adriatico, the milder alternative to tough, cold Paris-Nice. Tirreno-Adriatico, the 'race between two seas', gives the photographer or journalist a welcome chance to study the ever-mystical Italian racing scene.

Milan-San Remo, at nearly 300 kilometres and eight hours long, is an extremely difficult proposition in any

The race approached, sending a buzz of anticipation through the excited fans. Who would be first on the hill – Raas, De Vlaeminck, or perhaps even Freddy Maertens? They were on the cobbles now, the roar from the spectators below rising up to us. I could just see the leaders, between the rows of people craning like me for a clear view. A big man was in front, that much was certain, for his broad shoulders dwarfed the three or four cyclists in his wake. And now he was close – so close that, as he flashed by in his green Sanson jersey, oblivious to the steep gradient, I could establish his identity: he was the Italian, Francesco Moser.

Seeing this colossus in all his majesty – and on my first one-day classic – engendered in me the wish to discover more about this wonderfully refreshing sport. The following year I took my place on the same hill in the same race, and again it was Moser who led the way, showing a clean pair of heels to Michel Pollentier and Jan Raas. I was sufficiently hooked to cycle all the way, a few weeks later, to see the last cobbled section of Paris-Roubaix. I couldn't believe what my eyes were telling me: my hero Moser, coming this way, all alone in a cloud of dust and on his way to winning the race!

Since those early days, I've always had my eye on this champion, and he's never let me down: his powerful physique and imperious aura always make a good photograph. As the years have gone by, and my own experience has widened, I've realised how fortunate I was in those early sightings, for there are few enough champions of his class to enrich one's career. Now the sight of Moser – even off his bike – still draws my mind back to the Taaienberg, where the champion of Italy showed the partisan Belgians how it should really be done.

FRANCESCO MOSER

1 APRIL 1979: FLANDERS

The names of Dutch and Belgian cyclists were on everybody's lips as we waited in our thousands on the side of the Taaienberg for the imminent arrival of the Tour of Flanders. It was to be expected that the lowlanders should show the way in this, Belgium's foremost race – after all, people were saying, what other nations' cyclists know how to race over cobbled hills like this one?

circumstances; trying to cope with unfamiliar faces and jerseys as well makes it even tougher. If you are ready for it, however, Milan-San Remo can give you some of the best pictures of the season.

Race-day starts early – just after eight-thirty, with everybody lining up in the Piazza Del Duomo beside Milan's impressive cathedral that dwarfs everything around it. After bursting out of the suburbs at a furious pace, the race is split, pictorially, into two. First comes the Turchino Pass, reached after an uneventful 100-km approach across the Lombardy plains. On reaching the Turchino, with its snow-lined roads, the race favourites place themselves on the front of the bunch, forcing the pace up to an explosive tempo. Rarely is the road here

not banked by heaps of cleared snow, and the already photogenic faces of the riders turn increasingly more dramatic as the muddy slush is sprayed up off the road. At its summit, the photographer is suddenly aware that the season has really started; the first real – and perhaps the fastest – descent of the year speeds the usually intact field towards the city of Savona and the Mediterranean coast.

Milan-San Remo, 1983. Passing the peloton on the Capo Berta, I spotted a familiar figure in a Peugeot jersey. As we drew level our eyes met – Sean Yates looking in agony out of a mud-splattered face, mine through an 85 mm lens – and in that instant the shutter clicked

If the weather is favourable – and it usually is – the image of crazily coloured jerseys set against a backdrop of blue sky, blue sea and overhanging cliffs is a sight to behold and stays in our minds long into the season. It is here, on the long seaside section of the race, that we move into and alongside the strung-out peloton, creeping past at an ever-so-slightly faster pace to pick out individual riders, free of their winter clothing for the first time that year. Soon, however, we shall be shooed away by the race director who has little sympathy for our needs. For all of Italy's major races – those organised by the sports newspaper *La Gazetta dello Sport* – carry a distinctive trademark: Vincenzo Torriani. This legendary figure in Italian cycling, now in his late sixties, has long promoted and defended his races with a commitment and ferocity that will never be exceeded. Of all the race directors we encounter – and there are many – Torriani is the one who most strikes the fear of God into us with his appalling temper and unpredictability.

The second visual treat of Milan-San Remo occurs in the final fifty kilometres of the race: a string of short hills, culminating in the Poggio. This 4 km climb is the outstanding focal point of the race and the ultimate test for photographers. The last climb before the finish, its strategic importance is obvious; it is also the culmination of the three or four previous climbs, each of which adds to the pressure. As we approach the Poggio, the cauldron of our expectancy comes to the boil. We – and our drivers – will never be under more pressure during the whole season, knowing there's only one change of getting *the* picture. Nearly every modern *Primavera* victory has stemmed from an attack on the Poggio, and if, as is usually the case, nothing noteworthy has occurred up to this point, the nervous tension reaches an all-time high as the riders start the narrow, twisting climb. With Torriani standing up through the sun-roof of his car and screaming at us, it is important to

time one's move precisely. Any eight-hour race is very tiring, both physically and mentally, but by this stage in most races the result is already decided; where Milan-San Remo is tougher than most is that you must save the best of your concentration and nerve until the very end. Each photographer/driver team has its own plan, but one over-anxious move will lose you the game: you only get one chance.

The successful photographers are those who, with an almost telepathic insight, position themselves in the right place at the very instant that the attack comes – and it always comes – having assiduously evaded the murderous Torriani, who by now is hysterically ordering his chauffeur to drive at errant motorbikes. A few weeks later, when the colour magazines are published, a quick glance through the pages tells the story: who captured *the* moment, and who didn't. In 1988 we arrived at the foot of the Poggio having just witnessed a spectacular crash on the Cipressa and with most of my nervous energy already dissipated. As we manoeuvred for a good position the other, less committed photographers started to drive past, happy with a few shots taken before the real action began. For them, a steady drive to the finish, their work over: for us, a last-minute attempt to shoot the winning move followed by a heart-stopping descent into San Remo with the race-winner hot on our heels. Now there were only a few of us left: Cor Vos, Aldo Tonnoir, Denys Clement, George Rakič and myself, with not an Italian in sight. As the race approached the final kilometre of the climb *L'Equipe* driver Jacques Garcia took Clement into the fray, dropping back so quickly that Torriani had no time to react. There was only room for one at a time, so I decided to get in there when Clement had finished. I thought I'd got it right – for the first time in six years – for just as I dropped back, sustaining a punch from Torriani's driver, Van der Poel attacked, taking Erich Maechler and Laurent Fignon with him. We got right alongside the Dutch star as he

Adrie Van der Poel on the Poggio

A red rag and a bull! Vincenzo Torriani approaches boiling point

churned up the hill. I was content with about five seconds' work and told my driver Patrice to go; with the descent about to begin, I felt certain I had got the winning move. Off we went, but almost immediately I had my doubts: in all the confusion and stress, I had sent Patrice away without noticing that the other four photographers had resisted the temptation to evacuate the Poggio. At the finish, a kilometre from the foot of the descent, my worst fears were confirmed: Fignon came in to win, with Maurizio Fondriest a few seconds behind. A slowly-smiling Clement told me that Fignon attacked almost as soon as I had gone away.

Over the next few weeks I gradually collected all the other photographers' work. Fignon was on the front cover of all but one of the magazines, his strained features filling the page as he accelerated away with Fondriest glued to his wheel. Patrice and I both knew what it meant to miss the moment when Fignon went clear – Patrice too has his pride, and there are few opportunities for showing driving prowess to match the Poggio. Since then we've promised each other we'll get it right next time . . .

ERIC VANDERAERDEN

31 MARCH 1985: FLANDERS

The lone figure in front of us was unmistakable, curly blond hair streaming from under his sodden racing cap and, clinging wetly to his shoulders, the black, amber and red banded jersey indicating his status as champion of Belgium. In full flight along the roads of Flanders, Eric Vanderaerden was a compelling sight, and thousands of eager Belgians shouted enthusiastically from the roadsides as *their* champion rode by, on his way to an emphatic victory in *their* race: the Tour of Flanders.

Viewed through the torrent of mud-brown rainwater being flung off the road into our faces, this image of Vanderaerden is the one that stays with me. It is the legacy of a day when it poured with rain for over seven hours, at the end of which I had just one camera left working – and that without an exposure system. On such a day I needed a Vanderaerden to inspire me. He, of course, was impervious to all the discomfort; after all, this was his country, where racing in the rain is as natural as taking a bath.

If there is a 'bad boy' in the peloton it is Vanderaerden, his obvious and much-publicised cycling talent wasted by long spells of the apathy that frustrates even his most loyal supporters. To his supporters – myself included – Vanderaerden is a complete enigma, squandering a talent that could, if he wished, win him nearly all the one-day classics in the world, as well as the green points jersey in the Tour de France. But his very unpredictability makes watching him so exciting for those of us who have seen how good he can be: when Vanderaerden chooses to race, there is nothing to compare with him. Back arched low over the bike, hands draped along the tops of the brake levers, elbows at ninety degrees; gone the *prima donna* conceit that fame can bring to a Belgian professional, his sometimes arrogant face a study in determination of the rawest – and most attractive – kind. And when Vanderaerden explodes from the race to win events like the 1987 Paris-Roubaix, but most especially the 1985 Tour of Flanders, we know we are watching a superstar in flight.

The vicious ascent of la Redoute forced the very best out of Vanderaerden as he fought to stay in touch with the leaders. Liège-Bastogne-Liège, 1988

29

Tour of Flanders

Two weekends later, having got that first great race under our belts, the field of operations moves to Northern Europe – and particularly Belgium – for a month of the most action-packed racing available. The season is entering its spring classics phase: feared by some (the less ambitious Spanish and Italian teams), loved by a few – and a photographer's delight!

Belgium has, of course, a valid claim to be the premier cycling nation, with her long line of champions down the years. But it is her possession of more 'hors category' classics than any other nation that sets Belgium apart from her rivals. By the time we reach the Amstel Gold – the last true spring classic – we will have seen twelve national and international classics fought out on the exposed plains of Flanders and the beautiful hills of the Ardennes. And between these two regional rivals is the most fearsome race of them all: Paris-Roubaix.

Racing in this part of the world is a tough proposition: wind-swept plains, cobbled roads and tracks, and most of all, preponderantly miserable weather. But this series of races is the photographer's busiest time of year (the Tour de France excepted) and produces the most rewarding pictures. The riders are at their freshest – and therefore most competitive – and the photographer himself is operating flat-out for the first time, ready for anything and everything. It's virtually impossible not to capture some outstanding pictures; the landscape lends itself to drama before even a wheel is turned, and never more so than in the Ronde van Vlaanderen – the Flemish name for the Tour of Flanders.

They say that the character of the Flemish people is to be found in 'the Ronde' as it makes its way around the

Cobbles, mud and water: the essence of racing in Flanders

*. . . less than a minute later, Bauer, Kelly and Vanderaerden lead
the race over the Koppenberg — perhaps for the last time*

province. Lining the roads you see their impassive faces that mirror the hardships they and their families have endured down the centuries of war, conquest and never-ending struggle with the elements. Turning out in their thousands, dressed in their Sunday best, it's clear that this race means something special in a country where cycling is almost a religion. They wring every last ounce of satisfaction from this special day in their lives, using cars to criss-cross this most accessible of courses during its 276 km journey around their land. When they can no longer keep pace with the riders, they make for a café in which to while away the rest of the day, watching the race on television. And if it has been a Flandrian victory, they will celebrate well into the night. One look at the list of winners would indicate that considerable quantities of alcohol have been consumed since the first Ronde was held in 1913: only one non-Flandrian Belgian – Claude Criquielion in 1987 – has ever won Flanders, and there have been only eighteen foreign victories!

Although on a good day there is little to beat Flanders for the picturesque – the countryside around Eeklo and Aalter is particularly attractive, each turn in the road unveiling a fresh panorama, a windmill, a quaint canal bridge, a tree-lined avenue junctioned by a moated castle – the event is most notorious for its inexhaustible supply of cobbled climbs, or 'bergs'. The most famous of these 'walls' in recent history has been the Koppenberg, and it is here that photographers have had their best moments of the Ronde – and the cyclists their worst! During its twelve-year relationship with the race the Koppenberg always made for a great spectacle: thousands of spectators made the trip each year to this 600 m obstacle to see their heroes reduced to walking up the slippery, 25% slope. But for the riders it had long been regarded as an undignified farce, and its death knell sounded in 1987 when the Danish rider Jesper Skibby toppled over halfway up and was promptly run over by the race director's car! He was unhurt, but the ensuing bad publicity obliged the organisers to re-route the event for the following year.

Each year the sequence of cobbled hills alters in the search for the perfect route, but once they start – at around the 130 km mark – they come thick and fast: Molenberg, Oude Kwaremont, Pattersberg, Taaienberg, Eikenberg, Berendries, Geraardsbergen and finally the Bosberg – the main obstacles in an itinerary containing thirteen 'bergs'. And now the day's proceedings take on a very serious nature, and one very far removed from the fun and games of Milan-San Remo. At the end of the day, after seven hours spent being bumped and bounced around the countryside, squeezed off the narrow roads by service cars and generally pushed to the end of one's tether, it is a very tired photographer who waves goodbye to his colleagues until the next race.

Ghent-Wevelgem

As the crowds begin to disperse in Meerbeke after the finish of the Tour of Flanders, and the 'frites' stalls are dismantled, the mind turns to the prospects for the coming week.

Ask a photographer what Ghent-Wevelgem means to him and he'll probably tell you three things: the wind, the crashes and the Kemmelberg. For these factors have characterised this one-day race since the newspaper *Het Laatste Nieuws* decided to promote the race in 1934 as a way to provide cyclists with a preparation for Paris-Roubaix.

There's something pleasant about the predictability of Ghent-Wevelgem; pleasant, because it forms a less-demanding interlude between the difficulties of the Tour of Flanders and the hardships of Paris-Roubaix. It still takes place mid-week, attracting fewer spectators and less media attention than the weekend races; the race itself is easier to cover, as it is normally uneventful until

All hands to the rescue; policemen help Gilbert Duclos-Lassalle to his feet after his crash in the 1988 Ghent-Wevelgem, while beside him Bruno Leali has his own problems

we reach the tramlines: and the relaxed atmosphere enables us photographers and our drivers to socialise a little and enjoy the exquisite Flanders *paysage.*

So the working day in Ghent-Wevelgem begins in a carefully-selected cafe on the road to Knokke, the seaside resort through which the riders pass about two hours into the race. This untypical coffee-stop enables us to chat and laugh about the previous weekend's adventures and thrash out a tentative schedule for covering the big race at the weekend.

The Ghent-Wevelgem race-route has not changed much in all its long history, with the familiar journey out to the North Sea coast and the leg into the wind along the coast to Vuerne, where the race turns inland. It is here that the cross-wind takes its toll, dissecting the peloton into neat echelons for the thirty-kilometre thrash to Poperinge, where the hills begin to make their presence felt. Amongst these hills close to the French border waits the Kemmelberg, thirty-seven kilometres from Wevelgem and the focal point of the event.

But we join the race as it criss-crosses the tramlines of Zeebrugge and Oostende, and 200 cyclists are hopping like rabbits to avoid getting their wheels trapped in the two-inch wide tram tracks. Inexplicably, the pace has quickened to forty-five kilometres an hour, as if to inflict maximum damage – and provide us with those crash pictures we need to 'beef up' our portfolio of spring classics pictures. For it has to be said that the only reason we are there – standing up behind our drivers with cameras poised – is the hope of seeing a crash.

The side-wind leg along the N65 to Oostvleteren and Poperinge represents for me a very special occasion in my working year. As the races take me on a tour of Europe there are many breathtaking scenes – the Sierra Nevada in southern Spain, Val Gardena in the Dolomites, the Galibier pass in the Tour de France and the mountains of Connemara in Ireland's Nissan Classic – but none of these begin to compare with the thrill of seeing a peloton carved by the wind into echelons along this ordinary stretch of road in western Flanders. In 1983, when the wind was particularly cruel, it seemed as if a rider was falling at each passing kilometre, a bruising tumble into a rain-filled ditch the only option when the diagonal line of riders gets too long for the width of the road.

Yet in 1988, when a series of nasty crashes had left me deeply depressed, the same place had lifted my spirits. We had just sped away from the scene of yet another pile-up, and I was beginning to think I'd had enough. But soon we caught up to the bunch, just as the wind that had been in our faces became a cross-wind, wreaking havoc in the accelerating bunch. Suddenly the grey clouds parted and the sun came out in western Flanders, lighting the multi-coloured backs of these fearless gladiators as they danced with the wind, fighting for all they were worth in the wind-formed echelons that are such a feature of this race. Standing up behind my driver, viewing this extraordinary scene through a 180 mm lens, my spirits miraculously rose: 'Yes,' I thought then, 'I *am* happy to be doing this work.'

As we approach the Kemmelberg, five hours into the race, our attention is attracted at regular intervals to green-painted signs along the road. The route of Ghent-Wevelgem is a constant reminder that this land was a battlefield in the First World War: from Poperinge to the finish in Wevelgem we pass Kemmel, Wijtschat, Ypres, Zillebeke and Menen, the green signs indicating the position of so many war cemeteries, with one of the biggest memorials – to the French soldiers who fell there – at the foot of the Kemmelberg itself.

And so here it is: two climbs in one, since the race takes it in twice, in different directions. By the second time, forty kilometres later, the field is completely scattered and it is important to get off the hill as soon as possible, taking great care on the cobbled descent of the eastern side. Once safely down, there begins a high-speed chase to get up to the leaders before the officials organise themselves to stop us getting our precious pictures as the field attempts to repair the damage inflicted by the Kemmelberg.

It is here, on the road to Ypres, that some wonderful shots of this multi-rider pursuit match are to be had, including the obligatory picture as the race passes through the Menen Gate memorial in Ypres itself. It was here in 1985 that Britain's Joey McLoughlin first made a name for himself on the continent as he chased a super-fit Phil Anderson who was trying for a lone win in Wevelgem. But their escape failed, gobbled up by Dutch and Belgian sprinters out for a share of glory while they still had the chance – with Paris-Roubaix and the hilly classics looming, few opportunities remained for the pure sprinters to win a classic. Vanderaerden won that year, in a contentious sprint against his team-mate Anderson. This set the scene for the cobbles of Paris-Roubaix, where Vanderaerden, having won the Flanders a few days earlier, would be going for his third consecutive classic . . .

After the Kemmelberg, the next obstacle in the riders' working year is Paris-Roubaix – and the Wallers-Arenberg forest . . .

The wind, the sun, the gladiators: an echelon on the road to Poperinge

Dag-Otto Lauritzen took the Kemmelberg in his stride when he led the race over the first ascent in 1987

One of my favourite riders: Joey McLoughlin gives it everything on the Menen road in the 1985 Ghent-Wevelgem

Paris-Roubaix

Having survived one version of hell in Flanders, the prospect of another seven hours in what is commonly called 'the Hell of the North' ought to be a daunting proposition: the truth could not be more different. To the seasoned campaigner, Paris-Roubaix is the ultimate challenge in a year full of adventures. The public image of this race is of cobbled roads, mud-covered cart tracks and brave cyclists, struggling against the wind and rain, their muddy faces testifying to the ordeal they are undergoing. The photographer sees it this way too, but through this easily idealised surface poke the ugly specifics: the atrocious cobbles of the Wallers-Arenberg forest, the quagmire of a road near Ennevlin, and — most clearly of all — the black-mud surface of the tracks behind Camphin-en-Pévèle.

You know you'll get some cracking shots in Paris-Roubaix, but that's all you can be sure of in this most unpredictable of races. You may be soaked to the skin and have your cameras ruined: alternatively, if the race is run in dry conditions, you may have to swallow clouds of dust — and still have your cameras ruined! Both situations have their respective perils, though of course a wet day does guarantee considerably more drama — it's not even certain that you'll get to the finish! But that is part of the challenge of 'the Hell of the North'; after all, if the riders have to suffer, why shouldn't we?

To describe just the race-day of Paris-Roubaix would be like describing the ascent of Everest without mentioning the six-week-long approach march — for this one-day event means three days' work, including one full day's reconnaissance of the intricately complex route through the farmlands of northern France, in order to familiarise both driver and photographer with possible highlights and trouble spots. There is no easy way to get to know the course; even the most experienced photographers take the trouble each year to reconnoitre, for each year press cars and motorbikes get hopelessly lost, simply through lack of preparation. And it's not enough just to memorise the course; the roads and tracks are so narrow that even race-accredited photographers will have to make detours to get round the race.

The knowledge I've acquired from nine Paris-Roubaix — eight of them without official accreditation — gives me a distinct advantage: in those early days I had continually to divert away from the race, picking out only *the* best points to watch along the course, and — more importantly — how to get to them. Nowadays, with the prized 'plaque' on the motorbike, I can choose when to stay with the race and when to divert around it all. If either the race or the route is uneventful at points B and C, I know how to get directly from A to D, whereas other photographers are prisoners of the race route, not knowing where they are in relation to the outside world.

Race day dawns early, with an 8 am departure from my driver René's home in a Belgian village half an hour from the French border. We drive in the opposite direction to the race route, and passing through the villages of the Pas-de-Calais as they awaken to this race-day is a pleasant prelude to the rigours ahead.

As the first quarter of the race, from Compiègne to Le Cateau, is generally uneventful, we take up position where the race meets the first cobbles: in 1988, near the village of Troisvilles. Other photographers appear, and pleasantries are exchanged: all of us overtly at peace with ourselves, but inwardly tense — 'What's the race going to be like?', 'Have I got enough film?', 'Is it going to rain?', 'Will there be any crashes?', 'Will *we* crash?' . . .

Suddenly, here is the race director's red car, and the race is upon us. The cyclists cascade onto the cobbles like a swarm of rats, their faces showing all the tension I'm feeling as I fire away with my motor-drive . . . Soon they're all past, and all the other photographers scuttle

SEAN KELLY

13 MAY 1988: SEGOVIA, SPAIN

The nineteenth stage of the Vuelta a España, and a group of some twenty riders are starting the climb of Puerto de Navacerrada in the mountains to the west of Segovia. The 13 km ascent is the final climb in the 1988 Vuelta, but more importantly it is the last opportunity for race-leader Anselmo Fuerte to put time between himself and Sean Kelly, who would surely win the next day's stage against the clock, thus deposing Fuerte from the race lead.

So Kelly was expecting the series of moves that followed. Parra went first, almost as soon as the road began to rise seriously: Kelly responded immediately. Behind Kelly, Fuerte was watching . . . and waiting. Then Parra accelerated again: this time Kelly hesitated, waiting to see what Fuerte would do. It almost proved fatal, for just as Kelly looked behind him Fuerte launched a blistering attack on his other side, opening up a gap of fifty metres.

With the help of Robert Millar, however, Kelly soon had Fuerte back in his sights. Parra had a clear minute's advantage over Kelly, but the Irishman could have left it at that: Parra was no danger to him overall. He wasn't satisfied, though; tomorrow he could win the Vuelta in the time trial, but today he wanted to prove he was as good a climber as any in the race.

A fascinating pursuit developed, the lithe-limbed Parra versus the heavily-muscled Kelly – famous climber versus former sprinter. Through thousands of spectators these two extraordinary athletes raced until Kelly – with a posse of grimacing climbers behind him – had the Colombian in check. On the summit, the people cheered Parra over the top. Less than thirty seconds later, they cheered even louder as Kelly came into view, with Fuerte and ten others adrift, a mere sideshow to this wonderful display of strength and determination from the Irish legend. Kelly's face was set in its usual tight grimace, but his eyes had a look about them that said it all; Kelly had all but won his first-ever big national Tour.

This particular memory of Kelly is drawn from a decade of similarly stirring moments. Since the time I first photographed Kelly on the Champs Elysées in 1977 he has probably appeared in my sights more than any other cyclist: usually in victory, sometimes in defeat. It's the good times I remember best, and I'm proud to have seen all seven of his Paris-Nice victories and his hat-trick of Nissan International Classics. But Kelly's allure for a photographer doesn't begin and end with prominent racing moments, nor in the way his perched head and ramrod-straight body can be picked out instantly from a group of fifty riders. Like Hinault and Moser, Kelly has a distinctive aura about him which is impossible to define but which draws me like a magnet. As with all the greatest champions, there's that in Kelly's grey-blue eyes, icy as they are, that tells us something – but never everything – about his character. He is undoubtedly an extremely hard man, with a reputation for intimidating the most persistent interrogators, but amongst his trusted friends in the peloton there is another, and wickedly funny, side to Sean Kelly: dragging a can of Coke along the road to simulate the sound of a crash – a trick guaranteed to create pandemonium; or pressing the motor-drive button on some unsuspecting photographer's camera! We don't mind, for when he's smiling that winner's smile on the podium, the photographers smile too: Kelly is our favourite, our king.

'. . . bloody, but unbowed.' Sean Kelly, Paris-Roubaix, 1988

off to their motorbikes before the team cars can block their way – always stay ahead of the cars is the golden rule in this bizarre race. But we choose the opposite way, heading for a hill near Neuvilly; we arrive with a few minutes to spare and I fix my 300 mm lens to one of my cameras. Through the lens I can see Van der Poel and Bauer driving the bunch up towards us, their faces already grimy even though it's dry today. In the clouds of dust thrown up by 400 wheels only the front line of riders is visible, Bauer's clear sunglasses giving him the look of a surprised goldfish (but enabling him to see where he's going). Then we're off, and into the race . . . just until the next village, Solesmes, where we must divert again. I wink knowingly at fellow-photographer Aldo Tonnoir, travelling alongside: for us the race has really begun.

In the packed village the race swings right, towards the tracks waiting in the fields beyond. But we turn off, using our horn to clear a passage through the dense crowds. A cluster of press cars follows us through the gap, trying to get ahead for lunch in Valenciennes. We speed away, passed only by a CBS television car going flat out; we exchange nods with the Americans, each respectful of the others' commitment. Thirty minutes later we stop at an anonymous dip in the fields. I'd found a spot where the water still lay on the surface from a long-past rainstorm. 'There's bound to be a fall here,' I inform René, who's not really listening, since he is trying his best to keep the motorbike from sinking into the soft verge. Within seconds four or five other photographers pull up, with the same intentions.

Clouds of dust denote the arrival of the riders behind us. All too quickly they're past us, splashing through the muddy water. 'Another waste of time,' I mutter, peeved that as yet nothing of interest has happened. Then suddenly, a rider is in trouble: fighting to regain his balance, his front wheel slips on the mud and he somersaults into the ploughed field on his left. I sprint

over, eager to catch my first fall of the day, but he's too quick for me: he's regained the road and hopped back on his bike before I can get a decent shot at him. 'You're too slow!' laughs a woman who has been watching us. She was right, but I know as I run back to the motorbike that there will be other chances . . .

We chase after the race now, squeezing past the file of team cars that have worked their way up through the scattered riders. The wheels of the motorbike spin dangerously close to the ditch on our left as we pass each car. In the dust I can see no further than the front door of the Système 'U' car, just a few metres in front of us . . . my mouth is like sandpaper from breathing dust. Ten more minutes and we emerge from the fields into the outskirts of Valenciennes, and the day's second feed station; an opportunity to get past and onto the good roads that lead to the infamous Wallers-Arenberg forest.

Approached through the mining village of Arenberg, at first sight it is the dense plantation of tall ash trees, and the marsh from which they draw their life, that characterise this part of the race. But as you enter the forest the true hazard of the Wallers-Arenberg reveals itself: cobbles, tilting over in every direction, great gaps between them, differences in level of several inches . . . and in many places, no cobbles at all – just mud . . .

Riders can and do fall in the most unlikely places during Paris-Roubaix, and your chance of being on the one spot – out of sixty kilometres of *pavé* – where they choose to do it is slim. However, experienced photographers tend to hang around a particular stretch of the Wallers forest where many riders have crashed in past years. Here, the cobbles have all but sunk into the ground and the marsh has leaked into the vacant spaces. In 1984 Greg LeMond came to grief here, almost taking Sean Kelly with him. Kelly survived, but the fact that nine others had to divert into the undergrowth earned this spot considerable notoriety amongst the drama-seeking cameramen now assembled.

There's an air of expectancy as the race gets nearer, the buzz of the crowd hanging in the air of this natural cathedral. The lights from the escort motorbikes flicker as they make contact with the first cobbles, 500 metres from where we crouch. Suddenly they are here, forcing the spectators to jump back as they gather speed on the swoop into this tunnel of trees. Fignon judders by, his Cartier glasses seemingly glued to his nose, then Kelly, then a continuous stream of riders, vibrating visibly on the unyielding stones. It's more like watching a flickering home movie than a professional bike race.

There's only time for one good shot here, then René and I slither out onto the cobbles. Ahead of us lie another two jolting kilometres of cobbles, making even our 500 lb BMW twitch erratically. Every few seconds we are passed by chasing riders, using the grass verges to get by and save themselves further punishment, and we ourselves pass cyclists stopped by falls or punctures. Tempting as it is, we cannot stop, unwilling passengers on this cobbled travelator, cars before and behind us. Finally, like a dentist's drill that has done its painful work, the vibration of the *pavé* gives way to the gentle hum of tar-macadam and we reach sanctuary.

I relax, grateful for some respite from the bashing my nerves are taking on the slippery roads. Six riders – Peiper, Demol, Joho, Wegmüller, Van Rijen and Veldscholten – have got away and built up quite a lead. On one of the long sections of *pavé* between Hornaing and Sars-et-Rosières I stop and take a close-in shot of Allan Peiper as he leads the group along, knowing as they do that their moment of glory is unlikely to last; Kelly and sixty chasers are containing the four-minute gap.

We shuttle back and forth between leaders and chasers over the next thirty kilometres, getting increasingly frustrated at the lack of initiative shown by the favourites. I start to wonder if the leaders will really be caught, and try to think clearly who I have and have

not covered: plenty of shots of the leaders, but few of the favourites – Kelly, Bauer, Van der Poel, Fignon and Planckaert. And with the best of the cobbles still to come, I have to make a choice: follow the leaders, and miss out on the potential drama behind, or concentrate on Kelly's group and risk missing the finish.

I choose the latter course, and with forty kilometres of the race still to go we set off for the celebrated cobbles near Ennevlin. Here, after three kilometres of winding cobbled tracks, the road turns sharp left and suddenly disappears, engulfed by the surrounding verges, in which the press cars have gouged deep wells, wells that have now filled up with muddy water. It's the best thing I've seen all day and I shout excitedly at René to stop, much to the amusement of the crowds massed around the corner. I see that six or seven other photographers have done the same.

Almost before I'm ready the race arrives, with Bauer, tailed by Van der Poel and Planckaert, leading the chasers onto the track. The riders blur past where I crouch in the mud, focused on a large puddle and my reflexes ready for a fall there. All I see is the riders' eyes, blind to everything but the state of the road ten inches ahead of their front wheel. Incredibly, no one falls, though many come close, and I tear myself away to find the motorbike. To my horror I can see only a solid wall of people; I had not noted where René had parked the bike. Seeing the other motorbikes moving away with their photographers I start to panic, my desperate shouts for René lost in the babble of the spectators. At last I see his gloved hand waving to me from behind the crowds that have engulfed him, and barge frantically over to the motorbike.

We scramble out onto the track again, wedged between the KAS team car and the Roland car behind, but that momentary lapse on my part proves to be a disaster. Five seconds later, we all slither to a halt: 'Kelly est tombé!' I quickly dismount, struggling, like

A wet Paris-Roubaix produces the best pictures:
Eric Vanderaerden, 1985

the KAS team mechanic, to get a grip on the mud. I race the grey-haired mechanic to the scene, only to see Kelly back on his bike and being pushed down the road by his team-mate, Guido Van Calster. I curse the lost chance, but hurry back to René, still stuck where I left him. Incredibly, Kelly had fallen in the same spot the year before.

A few minutes later we regain good roads and speed on to catch up Kelly. Around the stricken Irish cyclist it's mayhem, with a dozen photographers working away; like me, they are aware that this could be the only drama of an otherwise indifferent day. We too get in on the action, albeit a little late. As I fire away I am saddened to see Kelly in this state, blood trickling down his temple, his dream of a third Paris-Roubaix lost in the mud of Ennevlin.

Thirty kilometres to go, and it's time to take our place on a cobbled corner in a hopeless maze of criss-crossing tracks I affectionately call 'the Bermuda Triangle'. For years Paris-Roubaix has acted out its final drama on these diabolical cart-tracks. There are sections where even the press cars are not allowed, the organisers fearful of them getting bogged down in the mud or having their sumps ripped away. For us too, the next forty minutes is a nightmare: we must leave the course three times in twelve kilometres, driving far too quickly on unsurfaced paths submerged in inches of water, haunted by the fear of missing the race at the next location.

We drive through the crowds on this 90° turn in the road, and I leave René, his engine still running, about thirty metres along a muddy lane. By the time I've found a good place in front of the spectators, the chasers are almost upon us; with so much excitement back at Ennevlin, the leaders have already passed through before we arrive. I leave the corner as soon as the first few riders have gone by; experience has taught me that a moment longer and our escape route may be blocked

Theo de Rooy, 1987. The black mud of Camphin-en-Pévèle claims another victim

as other people run for their vehicles. I run back to René and we set off at more than thirty-five kilometres an hour, despite the risks this involves. Behind us, a car full of journalists is hooting to get by, but I tell René to stay where he is, scared the car may force us into the ditch. In two kilometres we reach a T-junction in the middle of a ploughed field. Despite its remoteness, hundreds of people block our way through; seeing our 'official' motorbike, however, the gendarmes clear a path for us. The car behind is not so lucky; other parked cars have ended its involvement in this race.

By taking to the fields, we've bridged the four-minute gap between chasers and chased. The leaders arrive within ten seconds of me dismounting and I run off to

grab a few quick shots, only guessing the exposure in the time I've got. Now, instead of the dull features of fugitives awaiting inevitable capture I see the fierce determination of men who know they can win: heads lifted, eyes alert to their new status in 'the Hell of the North', going for all they're worth – I decide to stay with them. We accelerate past the four men – Veldscholten and Peiper have been dropped now, leaving DeMol, Wegmüller, Joho and Van Rijen to battle it out – and speed off on our next diversion, down an insignificant-looking path that takes us into the grounds of a magnificent chateau buried deep in a dark, eerie forest. Now there is just a kilometre between us and the most treacherous section of *pavé* in the race –

Camphin-en-Pévèle.

We get to the cobbles just as the television helicopter appears, its clattering blades hundreds of feet above proclaiming the arrival of the leaders. But disappointment awaits me; the cobbles that have for so many years satisfied the most crash-hungry photographers are today innocuously dry. Not so in 1987, where at this very spot I had witnessed the glorious sight of Eric Vanderaerden on his way to a fabulous victory, his cyclo-cross talent allowing him to race flat-out over the coal-black mud. Then, too, I'd seen some spectacularly horrid falls as riders lost their grip and fell head first onto the road, or toppled into ditches. And most startlingly of all, Sean Kelly covered from head to toe in thick black mud – a legacy of his fall at Ennevlin.

But today the sun is out, throwing a stark blade of light across the fields as the quartet approach. I focus with my 300 mm lens, needing a dramatic head-on shot to bring today's portfolio to life; it had been a mediocre day for photography, with such 'good' conditions and apathy amongst the favourites. Now, my luck is in – finally. The determined faces of Wegmüller and DeMol stare straight back at me, the 90° lighting lifting the group out of the shot, a cloud of dust acting as a magnificent back-drop.

With these good pictures safe, I decide to take a last look at the chasing group. They eventually appear three minutes later, confirming victory for one of the lesser lights in the quartet ahead, for now, surely, they wouldn't be caught. Moving off, however, we get caught amongst the dreaded team cars, and it is twelve kilometres before we can get past them. With our race radio out of action, a victim of the constant vibration, we have no way of knowing how far ahead the leaders are, or if there's been a change of order amongst the four. We finally catch sight of the trailing cars in the outskirts of Roubaix. We weave our way through to see that only two men remain in front: Wegmüller and DeMol. All

attention is focussed on Wegmüller's rear wheel, where a piece of plastic has entangled itself with the Swiss rider's gears, drastically reducing his chances of outsprinting his Belgian rival at the finish.

Into the last kilometre now . . . and here we must part company with the riders, as it is forbidden to work in this last section of the race. With just the formality of the finish left, I can relax a little: I have done all I can today – and survived. We pull into the finish area, where press officer Claude Sudres waits, ready to direct me to a vacant spot near the finish line. He's happy to see the photographers arrive safely – like a mother hen counting her chickens home – but still ticks me off for arriving at the finish so close to the riders: I am the last of the motorbike photographers to come in. A year earlier his sometimes suspect sense of humour had managed to survive when, without even official accreditation for a motorbike, I'd overtaken Vanderaerden inside the last kilometre in full view of the race officials. I shouldn't even have been on the route on a motorbike at all but couldn't bear to leave Vanderaerden in such fine form, so I had persuaded René – much against his better judgement – to throw caution to the winds and stay with him.

DeMol crossed the line, incredulous at his good fortune, and another Paris-Roubaix was over. So was my own ten-hour day; less challenging than previous years, and the result was a bit of an anti-climax, but later that night, after a good shower and an evening meal, as I drifted into a deep, deep sleep, I was thankful for a safe ending to an incredible adventure. What would it have been like if it had been wet . . .

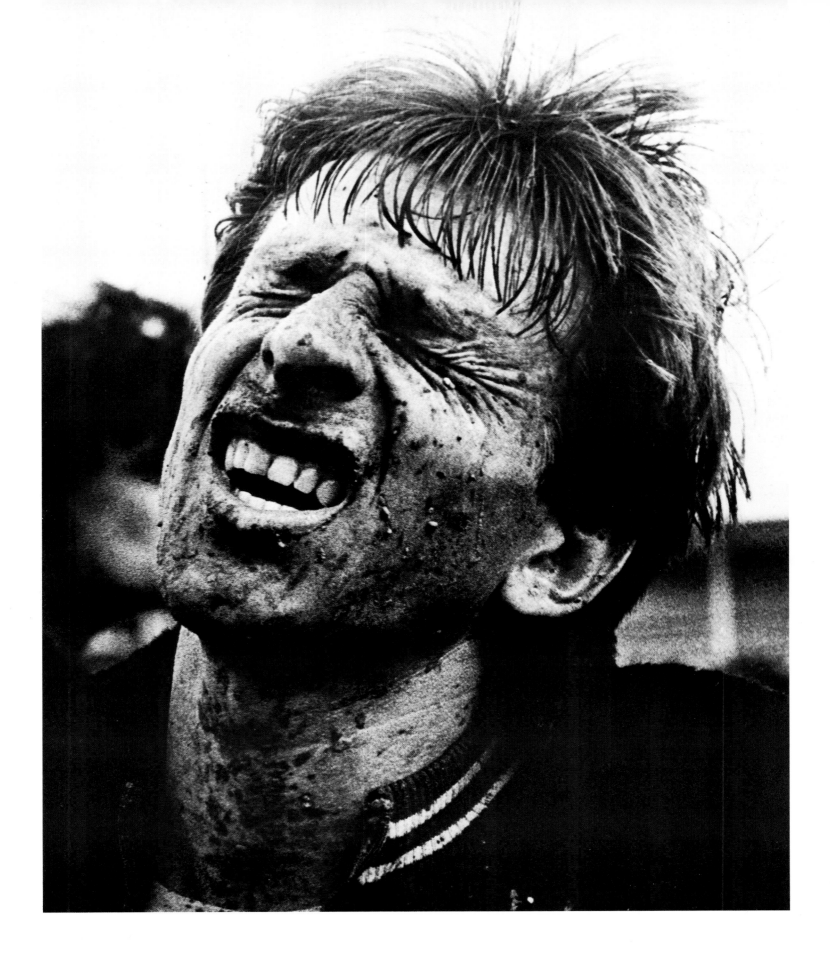

The Ardennes Classics: the Flèche Wallonne and Liège-Bastogne-Liège

Despite the nerve-jangling experience of Paris-Roubaix, it is in a nostalgic frame of mind that we ease ourselves out of the cobbled classics phase of the season and begin to consider the two great classics of the Ardennes – the Flèche Wallonne and Liège-Bastogne-Liège.

The days following Paris-Roubaix are spent in a trance-like state, as my mind churns over and over the memories of that day in the 'Hell of the North', cursing mistakes made and reliving the many highlights. The body, too, takes time to recover; my legs and back are so stiff that something as simple as bending to pick something up, or walking in a straight line, are very difficult at first. But it is the mind that takes longest to recover its normal awareness after the heavy demands made on your concentration. Paris-Roubaix leaves a lasting impression on both rider and photographer, making it hard to appreciate the forthcoming races which, whatever their merits, inevitably suffer from their position in the racing calendar. For Paris-Roubaix is the zenith of the spring classics, pushing distinguished events like the Flèche Wallonne into the background.

Nonetheless, what the 'Walloon Arrow' lacks in out and out racing it more than makes up for in its beautifully green landscape in the hills rising round the Meuse valley. There, in the vast forests of Bellegrange and Melard, with the hidden climbs of Ben-Ahin, Côte de Gives and Côte d'Ereffe, this enchanting race lifts us gently out of the lethargy that follows Paris-Roubaix and puts us in a competitive frame of mind, ready for Liège-Bastogne-Liège.

First run in 1892, Liège-Bastogne-Liège is the most senior of the world's 'hors category' classics and can flaunt an illustrious list of winners. Its race route shares many characteristics with its big brother in the north, the Tour of Flanders: eleven major climbs, and a similar race pattern, with a long first leg to Bastogne in Belgian Luxembourg followed by a gradual acceleration to the first real climbs near Stavelot, a sleepy walled town straddling the Amblève. From there, the climbs of Stockeu, Haute Levée, Rosiers, Maquisard, la Reid and Theux deliver the surviving cyclists up to the double obstacle of la Redoute and Côte des Forges, with just twenty downhill kilometres to Liège remaining, though the recently introduced Chaudfontaine climb drags the last ounces of strength from the leading riders before they finally reach Liège.

All these hills act like magnets on photographers, each one adding to the pressure as the race reaches its climax on la Redoute. La Redoute always plays a key role in Liège-Bastogne-Liège, its brutal climb out of the town of Remouchamps literally forcing a selection from the surviving riders. It was on this sheer hill, packed with spectators, that a television motorbike fell in 1985 while filming in front of the race. The drama that followed, with Phil Anderson's fall blocking the road, caused doubts about the race organisation, but for three riders – Roche, Argentin and Criquielion – it meant the chance to escape while the mess behind slowly cleared itself. That Argentin went on to win fuelled the argument, and the organisers were blamed for their failure to ease the congestion of the preceding press cars that stopped the motorbikes accelerating away.

The lackadaisical organisation of both Ardennes events is in stark contrast to the slick, professionally managed races of the north, where a knowledge of racing is part of the culture: inconceivable that they would have allowed the sort of accident that befell Liège-Bastogne-Liège in 1988, when bad communication meant that a local commissaire failed to position a roadside marshal on the descent into Houffalize. The result was that the entire 200-man bunch, speeding at seventy kilometres an hour towards the first feeding station, ploughed into a stretch of road under repair by

A tapestry of green fields and forests in the background, the leading break in the 1988 Flèche Wallonne wends its way over the Côte des Gives

The current notoriety of Liège-Bastogne-Liège owes much to the exploits of Bernard Hinault, seen here stretching the legs of René Bittinger and Johan Van Der Velde on the Haute Levée in 1983

In 1983 Steven Rooks added his name to the star-studded list of Liège-Bastogne-Liège winners

workmen. More than fifty riders fell, many suffering serious leg injuries, and Laurent Fignon was out of the race with multiple abrasions. A week later, still unable to race, Fignon threatened legal proceedings against the organisers.

If these setbacks have tarnished the reputation of the race, its most characteristic feature has not changed at all. Throughout its long life, the fickle climate of Europe in mid-April has invariably dumped its foulest weather on Liège-Bastogne-Liège, and never more so than in 1980. In that year, on a day that would have kept all but the really foolhardy at home, Bernard Hinault wrote his name indelibly in the annals of cycling with one of the greatest displays of courage and stamina the race has ever seen. Many experienced French and Belgian photographers still recall with relish the story of Hinault's epic ride when, after a counter-attack on the Stockeu 'wall', he rode the last ninety kilometres, over the eight remaining climbs, through a horrendous snowstorm, alone. Despite being frozen to the marrow, the twenty-four-year-old Breton arrived in Liège with an incredible eight-minute advantage. For one photographer in particular, Henri Besson, that day rates with any in twenty years of following races on the back of a motorbike. Hinault's performance that year is the outstanding memory of a decade of Liège-Bastogne-Liège, and did a great deal for the reputation of this great race at a time when it most needed it.

Apart from the incidents on la Redoute in 1985 and the crash in 1988, Liège-Bastogne-Liège lacks the unpredictable drama of races like Milan-San Remo and Paris-Roubaix, having more in common with the Tour of Flanders, both events being decided by a process of elimination rather than a clear-cut moment which decides the issue. But while Flanders has its cobbled hills, Liège-Bastogne-Liège is indisputably winner in the matter of bad weather; and nobody now can ever reflect on this without remembering the name of Bernard Hinault.

Five years on, his smile says it all: Yates wins the Jaca stage of the 1988 Vuelta

SEAN YATES

19 MARCH 1983: THE ITALIAN RIVIERA

When you're in your first professional season and riding in your first real classic, a relatively miniscule hill like the Capo Berta in Milan-San Remo can have the nastiest effect on your diminishing reserves of stamina. That's how Sean Yates came to remember his baptism into big-time racing, having neglected the opportunity to collect a food-bag at the final feeding station, twenty kilometres before.

I was inching my way past the heaving peloton on the Capo Berta when I caught sight of a bulky figure wearing a Peugeot jersey – unmistakably Yates. As I passed our eyes met: mine squinting through an 85 mm lens, his out of a face screwed up in agony and exhaustion. It was a short exchange – I couldn't bear to look at him in such a state,

when a few weeks earlier, posing for a pre-season picture in the lush setting of his native Ashdown Forest in Sussex, he had been so fresh-faced and happy.

But Sean Yates has come a long way since then, winning stages in the Vuelta and Tour de France, and leading the 1988 Paris–Nice for four days. At the same time he has become a most popular rider, respected by both the press and his colleagues. It's no coincidence that his best mate in the peloton is Allan Peiper; entirely different physically, they still share the same fierce passion about their racing. Also like his Australian friend, Yates is entirely unselfish as a rider, and as a consequence has had fewer wins than he is capable of – which bothers him not at all! Refreshingly, in a sport that is coming to be dominated by commercial interests, he doesn't go courting publicity, and thrives on the supporting role he plays best: his awesome strength can help team-mates do well in situations where he himself cannot. At the same time, he can enjoy using that power to string out a Tour de France peloton in his wake at forty miles an hour, teasing them with the threat that one day, if he wants, he will leave them all behind.

His physical dimensions – six feet two, twelve stone and hands like a lumberjack's – might indicate the presence in the peloton of an ungainly bully. But his good riding manners and mild disposition preclude any such possibility: instead, he diverts his surplus competitive drive into trials riding, dinghy sailing and rock climbing – at the moment . . .

When Yates clocked the fastest time to date in the time trial stage to Wasquehal in the 1988 Tour de France, and had to wait nearly two hours to find out if anyone could beat it, television viewers saw a shy, reserved man trying to come to terms with the fact that he, and not a Fignon or Bernard, had won a strategic stage of the Tour. All of a sudden, the man who had writhed in agony on the Capo Berta five years before was within fourteen seconds of the yellow jersey!

Spot the riders: the summit of the Gulpenberg packed with spectators in the 1988 Amstel Gold

The Amstel Gold

By the time the Amstel Gold, Holland's only international one-day race, comes along on the last weekend in April, many teams will have left for the Vuelta a España, the first of the three big national Tours, leaving a smaller field to contest this comparatively new race. The Amstel Gold is different from the other spring classics in two other ways: under instructions from the police, the organisers restrict the numbers of press cars and motorbikes to a minimum – only six motorbike photographers are given access to the race. And unlike all the other major races in mainland Europe, the roads are not completely closed to traffic for the race, which means we must adopt a more cautious attitude to travelling ahead of the race for coffee – only as the race actually approaches do road users pull over for a few minutes.

The race is held in the stunningly pretty Limburg region, the tear-drop-shaped corner in the south, surrounded by West Germany and Belgium. Holland is hardly noted for its hills, but the main features of the Amstel Gold are the major climbs of the Gulpenberg, the 'König van Espanje', and the incredibly steep Keuternberg – 500 metres of 25 per cent hill including a section of 28 per cent! These hills (and there are up to fifteen of them), and the final Cauberg, are where all the action happens in this modestly-proportioned event. Its intricately wiggly 245 kilometres never gets further than 45 kilometres from its start at Heerlen and finish at Meersen, its compact characteristics designed by the organisers to give the sports-mad Dutch public a real chance to come out and enjoy the race, which they certainly do. And since they pass the time waiting for the race to come along in bars and cafes along the route, the scenes on the Gulpenberg, Keuternberg and Cauberg can be quite startling. 'Watch out for drunken Dutchmen', mutters my Belgian driver whenever anyone mentions the Amstel Gold!

By and large, the Amstel is a predominantly Dutch affair, and few foreigners attempt to break the stranglehold. But in 1983 Phil Anderson did just that, romping away with veteran Joop Zoetemelk in the lanes approaching the Cauberg climb out of the mediaeval town of Valkenburg. And when the Australian dropped Zoetemelk on that very climb it was not at all to the taste of the thousands of Dutch fans swarming all over the road. On the descending roads to the finish in Meersen the race officials, determined to make sure that Anderson received no undue assistance, prevented any

motorbikes from working in front of him. Our only option was to divert on to the cycle-path that ran parallel with the road and get some pictures that way. Thus it came about that a six-man group of training cyclists coming from the opposite direction found themselves suddenly confronted by three big motorbikes travelling at sixty kilometres an hour!

The only difficulty of working on the Amstel Gold is that the race travels through some places, like Valkenburg, two or three times, which can be confusing: carrying a good map on race day is the only precaution you can take against getting hopelessly lost. In general, though, the Amstel Gold is a pleasant way to close the spring classics and prepare for departure to Spain and the first big national stage race . . .

Phil Anderson exuding elation on winning the Amstel Gold in 1983

PEDRO DELGADO

21 JULY 1988: MASSIF CENTRAL, FRANCE

For the best part of a week, the Tour de France as a race had been paralysed by the 'did he, didn't he' drug rumours about Pedro Delgado. The riders, the press, indeed the whole Tour entourage was desperate for reassurance that the Tour de France was still what it had always been – a great *sporting* occasion.

All of us felt let down by the sloppy organisation that failed to confirm or deny the rumours, making it impossible to judge the racing with any conviction. Nobody had more reason to feel let down than Pedro Delgado; all he wanted to do was get on with winning the Tour and refute the slur on his reputation. The steep slopes of the Puy de Dôme were the ideal outlet for his frustrations.

By the time the real stars entered the stage the day's top honours had already gone to Johnny Weltz and Rolf Gölz. Steven Rooks, Gert-Jan Theunisse and Pedro Delgado filled the screen in my viewfinder as they rode abreast into the final three kilometres of the mountain. The likeable Spaniard was out to make a point in the best way possible – he had determination written all over his handsome face, liquid brown eyes intent on the road ahead: no-one was going to take this race away from him!

Rooks cracked first under the pressure, and the face of Theunisse betrayed the effort he was making just to stay with Delgado; with less than two kilometres to go, he knew his turn was next. A barely discernible dip in his shoulders, a tensing of his quadriceps, and Delgado was gone – not looking to the right or left, just straight ahead. I wanted to record this symbolic moment and we tucked in behind Theunisse; with every passing metre Delgado drew further away, his splendidly-defined leg muscles pumping more power onto the pedals. Away he went, like an uncaged lion.

The huge crowds loved this bravura performance in defiance of the opprobrium that was being heaped on the wearer of the yellow jersey. And Delgado was loving it too, turning on more and more power as he neared the realisation of his ambition: there was more to this performance than simply proving that he *was* the best cyclist in the Tour de France . . .

When Delgado rode into Paris as the overall winner, all but a few sulking French journalists applauded his victory. It was recognised as a well-deserved honour for a deservedly popular cyclist. Spain's most popular sportsman by far – the regard in which he is held now approaches worship – 'Perico', as he is known, has proved that he is a worthy representative of a country whose people are famous for the importance they attach to honour.

This attack by Delgado on the way to la Plagne in the 1987 Tour de France pushed Stephen Roche to collapse. Taking the shot from such a low angle (the ditch!) highlights the intensity of his effort

La Vuelta

Just a few days after the Amstel Gold, a plane touches down at Bilbão's international airport. For the cycling photographer on board there is more to the flight than the one and a half hours' flying time. The journey to Spain in late April means an abrupt transition from one-day races to stage racing: the Vuelta a España, the first of the three great national Tours that form the heart of the racing season.

Working a stage race so early in the season is quite a challenge, coming as it does when the mind is still attuned to the thrills and spills of the classics. In Spain, those one-day adventures will be replaced by the rigours of stage-racing and all it entails: long, sometimes arduous days containing nothing of interest; endless searching each evening for hotels and then for mislaid baggage; sharing rooms with complete strangers; eating late or sometimes not eating at all; living out of a suitcase for weeks on end. In the racing, gone is that compelling excitement that builds up to a crescendo in a single-day event when you know there'll be an outright winner. In a stage-race there seem to be only three or four days when anything of consequence occurs, and even then – such is the chess-like nature of stage-racing – it's unlikely that the final outcome will be known till the very end.

This way of life will last for the best part of the next three months: the Vuelta is followed almost immediately by the three-week-long Giro d'Italia and a few weeks later by the big daddy of them all, the Tour de France. Needless to say, despite all the inconveniences the national Tours offer considerable attractions, not least of which is the opportunity to soak up the culture and way of life of each country. People, landscape, architecture, cuisine: it is for these reasons that the Vuelta a España is such an attractive assignment.

On an international scale both the Vuelta and the Giro are less important than the Tour de France, and are therefore supposed to play a supporting role by preparing the best riders in the world for the French race. Whilst it is hard to argue with that proposition, the Vuelta finishes more than six weeks before the Tour begins, so it is probably more accurate to assign that role to the Giro. Also, of course, the Vuelta is so tough that anyone hoping to win it must virtually abandon all hope of finishing well in the Tour de France.

If stage racing, then, is quite unlike single-day competition, so too the Vuelta cannot be seen as a 'typical' Tour. The Vuelta abides by few of the traditions maintained by other cycling nations, both as regards the racing and the organisation. It could be said that the Vuelta is as much an expression of the Spanish character as a bike race, such is the vibrant way the race winds its way round the country. And cycling in Spain is so popular that the Vuelta could quite well survive without the involvement of foreign riders and teams; Pedro Delgado's win in the 1988 Tour de France crowned a decade-long revival of interest in the sport. That foreigners do participate, however, makes the Vuelta even more competitive and this element of competition communicates itself to the Spanish people. 'La Vuelta' is for them, *los aficionados,* and they show it by lining the streets ten-deep, chanting and clapping the riders through each and every village along the route. And when the race comes to a big town such as Burgos in the north, or Granada in the south, the people are there in their hundreds of thousands – literally! – crowding the pavements when they can and, when there's no more room to be had on the ground, hanging out of the windows and balconies of their twenty-storey apartment blocks.

The size and exuberance of the crowds is the most significant feature of the Vuelta; even the massively popular Tour de France fails to match it in this respect. Covering the Vuelta means working an extra shift after

The ancient town of Toledo, every inch of balcony alive with spectators, gives an enthusiastic welcome to Malcolm Elliott as he wins this prestigious stage in 1988

A light-hearted moment as riders congregate before the start of a stage

the racing has finished. As each stage arrives in town for its overnight stop, the population goes wild, staging open-air discotheques or dancing and singing in the streets, and for everybody on the race there's no such thing as an early night. Within hours of the finish the bars and cafés begin to fill with the Vuelta's entourage of Spanish and foreign press, organisers and sponsors, mixing with the locals and drinking their way through the evening before seeking out a restaurant at about midnight. It doesn't end there, either; in the early hours – when even the locals are fast asleep – the entourage heads for the discotheques, dancing and singing until three or four o'clock in the morning. Such is the warmth and hospitality of the Spanish people that you cannot resist joining in with their merry-making. Repeated every night, however, it can begin to take its toll, and you have to call a halt to regain some lost sleep. The hectic lifestyle doesn't seem to have the same effect on the motorbike drivers, who often stay out all night bolstering up their machismo. Towards the end of the 1988 Vuelta, after a stage to Albacete, Ismael, my driver from San Sebastian in the Basque country, bid me 'adíos' at around seven in the evening. Grateful for the rare chance of an early night, I went to bed at ten o'clock, and slept until seven-thirty next morning when I was woken by the sound of Ismael moving around. Thinking he was getting dressed, I was shocked to see him get *into* bed – he'd been out all night! Barely an hour later we were on our way to the start, with the prospect of a mountainous 140 kilometres ahead of us . . .

The anarchic mood of the Vuelta affects the racing too, sometimes flat out in the first few hours for no apparent reason, or letting a series of modest riders win the days between the numerous mountain stages. The one area where the race does follow tradition is in the mountains – and in this respect Spain has no equals. Its vastness is well supplied with mountain ranges; some, like the Pyrenees, familiar to all and therefore easy to anticipate, whereas the Cantabrica mountains south-west of Santander contain many unexpectedly vicious ascents. It was here in 1985 that I had my first taste of the Vuelta, watching spellbound as the road climbed sharply out of the Sella valley into the Covadonga National Park, an area normally closed to cars to protect the wilderness and wild animals that live there. After a 20 km slog through pine forest, up to a lush green plateau and then – at nearly 2,000 metres – excruciatingly up again, on the narrowest and twistiest of roads, the stage finished at Lagos de Covadonga, a cluster of shepherds' huts and two crystal-clear lakes below the glacier-covered mountains of the Picos de Europa. To this day I have never seen a more beautiful and more unimaginable setting for the finish of a race.

Following a race by motorbike must be one of the best ways to see any country, particularly one as rich and beautiful as Spain. Historical cities like Aranjuez and Segovia are regular points of interest along the route, as are Seville, Cordoba and Granada in Andalucia. Wherever the Vuelta finishes each day, another chapter of Spanish history unfolds; well away from the tourism of the Mediterranean coast, in fifteenth-century Toledo or tenth-century Avila in the very heart of Spain, the beauty of the country is completely unspoilt. One of the strategic landmarks of the Vuelta is the Sierra Nevada, its flat-topped, 2470 metre snow-covered mountains dominating the skyline for seventy kilometres around, its summit only reached for the riders after a gruelling 35 km climb.

Each year the Vuelta finds new routes to race, including the Balearic islands off the Costa del Azahar and the more distant Canaries, from which in 1988 Sean Kelly launched his victorious campaign. But the Vuelta is more at home on the exposed prairie of La Mancha, the rugged Galician region in the extreme north-west, the rolling hills of Catalonia and – perhaps most of all – Andalucía, Spain's best-loved province and home of the

The mountainous Vuelta is well suited to the climbing talent of Spanish cyclists like Alvaro Pino and Laudelino Cubino, seen here climbing Estación Cerler. Behind them, foreigners Parra and Millar have other plans . . .

most beautiful girls. In 1986 the Vuelta reached its conclusion in Jerez, near the historic sea-port of Cadiz from which four centuries ago the Armada set sail to conquer England. On this day, however, there were no hostilities. Instead, on the sweeping descent from the hills of Ronda, just a mutual appreciation with my driver of the view across the Straits of Gibraltar to where the mystical mountains of Morocco poked through the sea-mists into a deep blue sky . . . under the influence of scenes like these the cold and wet of the spring classics finally fade from the mind.

On the Passo Duran during the Giro d'Italia. Using a long lens from a motorbike brings Hampsten out of the group, enhancing his dominance

ANDY HAMPSTEN

10 June 1988: Passo Duran, Italy

The 1601 m high Passo Duran, near Cortina in the Italian Dolomites, is extremely steep. Six kilometres from the top it becomes unsurfaced, and therefore extremely difficult. Hardly a place where one expects to engage the wearer of the *maglia rosa* in conversation, and certainly not when he's having to contend with a timely attack designed to relieve him of that precious pink jersey. But that's what happened on the last mountain stage of the 1988 Giro d'Italia.

Urs Zimmerman had attacked lower down the climb and accumulated a lead of more than two minutes, and I dropped back to film Hampsten's reaction, expecting to see the lithely-built American in a state of some anxiety. So I

was staggered, as I hovered in front of him, to hear him calmly ask: 'Hey Graham, is it just Zimmerman who's up there?' Recovering from my surprise (was he really talking to me?), I replied that Zimmerman was indeed alone – and resisted the temptation to continue the conversation. With Zimmerman still pulling away – his lead increased to a massive seven minutes later in the day – I just hoped Hampsten knew what he was doing.

Fortunately, Hampsten and Jeff Pierce – the only one of his team-mates able to stay with him on the climb – stayed cool and waited for the arrival of second-placed Eric Breukink and his Panasonic team. They would make it their business to bring Zimmerman to heel, Hampsten knew, which was why he didn't appear worried. And he was right; by the end of the day, Zimmerman's lead had been reduced to the point where he was no longer a threat to Hampsten.

That incident is typical of Hampsten's coolness under pressure, which will be a huge asset when, as expected, he goes for his first Tour de France win. Accused by some of being moody and temperamental, Hampsten seems to me instead to have achieved a grace under pressure that you normally only see in more experienced athletes. I realised that day how much he'd matured since his first big victory in Europe, a stage win in the same event in 1985. Then, Hampsten's team leader, Bernard Hinault, had referred to the American as 'our little rabbit' – a reference to Hampsten's prominent front teeth. Hampsten is not a man to exhibit animosity, but he must have got some satisfaction from helping Greg LeMond beat Hinault a year later in the Tour de France. Since then he has grown in confidence – and had an operation to realign his front teeth.

As a photographer, one has to wait for the spring and summer stage races to capture a finely-tuned rider like Hampsten at his best. When he takes off in the mountains where he feels so much at home, it's a joy to watch. Climbing out of the saddle, his long, thin arms and upper body rigid to allow just his legs to jig the bike forward; then, when he's not attacking, he sits down and spins a small gear, saving his energy for another attack. On and off the bike, Hampsten's clean-cut looks, fitness and notable good manners reflect his open-air, mountain background in Boulder, Colorado, which stood him in good stead for the Dolomites – and for holding a conversation at the same time!

*The camera does lie; this
arrogant mask is untypical
of Andy Hampsten,
but it makes a great picture!*

Giro d'Italia

Italy in June is very different from the Italy we last encountered in March for Milan-San Remo, when the action-packed sprint across the chilly plains of Lombardy gave us little chance to savour this beautiful country. Its hibernation over now, the countryside is blossoming, from the olive groves of Venezia to the mimosa-strewn hillsides above Lake Garda, with, towering above it all, the rocky pinnacles of the Dolomites.

The racing image of the Giro d'Italia derives from the Dolomites: the stunningly beautiful Val Gardena, with its tall spires of rock projecting high into the skies from grassy meadows and thick pine forests, and the Passo Stelvio in the Alps, that has witnessed the most infamous moments of the Giro's history. The Giro nearly always terminates in these mountains, their topography of great value in securing a verdict from the favourites still in with a chance of winning the race (and far more accessible to us foreigners, who only cover the last twelve days or so!)

As a race, the Giro can often be dull: for the most part, the *corredori* ride *en-masse,* only bestirring themselves when the television helicopter appears overhead, signalling the start of live transmissions. Even in the mountains the confrontation with gravity and altitude is deferred as long as possible. But working on the Giro can be quite exciting: the legendary hostility of the Italian *tifosi* seems also to infect the riders, a fact which may explain why a foreigner didn't win the Giro until its thirty-fourth year. Since then, the Giro has been won by foreigners twenty times in thirty-eight years, including five by Eddy Merckx and three by Hinault. Merckx rode for an Italian sponsor, and the *tifosi* have gradually learnt to accept a foreigner winning as long as they can regard his victory as worthy of their national tour – and as long as it doesn't entail defeating a worthy Italian. Andy Hampsten's victory in 1988, against weak opposition and some atrocious weather, earned their respect, but the way Stephen Roche went about winning the 1987 Giro seriously threatened this entente.

That year, I was the only non-Italian photographer working on the race, and the fiercely partisan Italian press, to say nothing of the jeering, pushing, spitting *tifosi,* reinforced my natural inclination to sympathise with Roche's predicament. It seemed that half of Italy was at his throat, but I just managed to curb these instincts in the interests of professionalism and impartiality!

I shall never forget the tension in the air the day after he 'pirated' Visentini's lead; Stephen Roche in the *maglia rosa* doggedly climbing the fearsome Marmolada against a tidal wave of emotion, Robert Millar and Eddy Schepers riding shotgun on either side to fend off physical attack. When Visentini launched a futile attack the accompanying press motorbikes dropped all semblance of discipline and the scene degenerated into a free-for-all as motorbikes collided and photographers fought – literally – for the best position. Blows were exchanged between the television driver, struggling to keep his plum position, and some of the other drivers, struggling to usurp it, turning an already ugly scene into a dangerous one, heavy bikes weaving all over the road on the steep incline.

Strangely, our old adversary Torriani maintained a passive profile throughout; pleased, perhaps, at the publicity his race was receiving.

But incidents like these are outside the normal pattern of working on the Giro: ordinarily there is *less* tension than in other events, and the relaxed atmosphere, warmer weather – the first chance in the season to wear summer clothes – and Italian informality make life on the Giro a pleasure. Inevitably, though, this informality has its down-side, particularly in the organisational sense.

Fearful conditions, like these on the Passo Rambo, made the 1988
Giro d'Italia memorable – in more ways than one!

In 1988 I'd arranged for an Italian driver to be at the start of the fourteenth stage from Chiesa Valmalenco to Bormio, via the famous Gavia Pass. The morning was wet and cold as I came down for breakfast in the Toshiba team's dining room (my room *had* been intended for a Toshiba rider, but he had quit the race the day before and his misfortune had been my good luck: a shortage of rooms is another feature of life on the Giro!) I saw that the team was dressed for the worst possible weather: word had spread through the town that snow had fallen on the Gavia during the night.

As the race prepared to leave town an hour later, I waited in vain for my transport. Apparently the driver I had requested had not yet been contacted by the people in charge: I couldn't find a journalist willing or able to give me and my luggage a lift, so when the race set off for Bormio it left behind one very disgruntled Englishman standing in the rain with two hefty bags and a pile of camera equipment. On any other day, I would easily have found a place in one of dozens of press cars: as I was later to discover, however, this was not going to an ordinary day . . . Eventually, I managed to hitch a lift with a female soigneur on the 7-Eleven team, who was avoiding the Gavia and driving directly to the finish in Bormio.

Rain was still falling heavily as I went to the finish line in Bormio, lucky – on the face of it – to have escaped a freezing cold day on the back of a motorbike, but inwardly cursing at what I knew in my bones was a lost chance. This sinking feeling intensified as the TV monitors showed the awful conditions. Somehow a television helicopter had got up above the Gavia in the storm and was beaming its pictures down to Bormio, and the screens were filled with an Andy Hampsten rendered barely recognisable by the conditions and his soggy clothing.

When the race finally arrived, the full awfulness of the conditions – and my missed chance – became apparent. Eric Breukink won the stage a few seconds ahead of the American, but no motorbike photographers accompanied them, and I ground my teeth as I realised that they had stayed up on the Gavia and were getting some very special shots indeed. I did what I could, shooting some horrific scenes as each pathetic figure wheeled into the finish area, to collapse in a state of near-hypothermia. I have never seen grown men in such a state, with the likes of Pedro Delgado and Urs Zimmerman trembling uncontrollably, as though they were having an epileptic fit, and America's Bob Roll collapsing and being carried away for medical attention.

The next morning I couldn't bear to listen as the other photographers gleefully related their experiences. I had something in the way of 'hard' pictures, but they had something to treasure: photographs that would still provoke an awed reaction in twenty years' time, recalling the frightful conditions of that famous day on the Gavia.

Thereafter, apart from one particularly concentrated attack on Hampsten's lead, the Giro resumed its typical less than frantic tempo, a gentle meander towards Venice under a warm sun easing some of the painful memories. Down the years, the Giro has experienced occasional spasms of controversy and excitement, interwoven with racing that photographers remember for its long, boring *promenades*, balmy weather and relaxed atmosphere. The latter is an important factor for those of us who have been on the road virtually non-stop since early February and will be in France the following month; we have to make the most of this *séjour*, for there'll be little enough chance to relax on the Tour de France.

A typically aggressive shot of Phil Anderson in the 1988 Tour of Flanders

PHIL ANDERSON

22 JULY 1987: THE FRENCH ALPS

Of all the hairy descents in the mountains of the Tour de France, the north side of the Col du Galibier is one of the hairiest. At least, that's how it seemed to me as my driver and I descended from the 2556 m summit several minutes after the leaders had gone through. The view from the top of the high pass had been magnificent, and I felt at peace with the world amid the snow-clad peaks of the Grandes-Rousses: but not for long. About five kilometres down the corkscrew road a blue and white jersey swooped past, catching us off-guard with his speed. I identified him immediately – black crash-hat, black Oakley sun-shades and large gleaming teeth – it could only be Phil Anderson.

It was risky, but we decided to follow this notoriously crazy descender, maybe play a game with him, for he was clearly enjoying himself after the ordeal of the climb. The game started well for us, and we stayed with him on a long straight where cyclist and motorbike reached over 100 kilometres an hour. My driver even took me past so I could record this bizarre race, but it was no use: at that speed my eyes were watering too much for me to get anything worthwhile.

Now it was Anderson's turn; at the start of a series of bends six kilometres from the bottom he swept past, his athletic body confidently taking him into and through the unending hairpins. It was an enviable sight; well-muscled legs – larger and more clearly defined than most cyclists' – and his upper body aimed like a bullet at the descent, all against a background of alpine meadows and distant snowy peaks: the ultimate example of a man at ease with his bike.

We played our final card, accelerating past two kilometres before the town of Valloire, but Anderson was having none of it. Now descending at nearly 110 kilometres an hour, he sprinted out of the saddle in his biggest gear and drew close to our back wheel. A few hundred metres and he'd won the game: a sweeping right-hander on the approach to the town forced us reluctantly to concede. I sighed in acknowledgement of his courage and skill as he executed a perfect passing move at nearly eighty kilometres an hour – on our inside . . .

Even when he's not entertaining the photographers with his bike-handling skills, Phil is one of the most highly regarded cyclists in the peloton. This regard dates back to his early years as a pro when, undaunted by Hinault's powerful presence, Phil – almost alone amongst the peloton – had the temerity to challenge his pre-eminence; in the 1981 and '82 Tours de France, this Australian achieved the honour of wearing the yellow jersey for a total of eleven days. He has courage, a splendidly photogenic physique and a never-say-die attitude to racing: his presence in the peloton makes our job worthwhile. If only he'd take off those Oakleys!

Tour de France, 1987: Luis Herrera prepares to take off on l'Alpe d'Huez, leaving Roche (hidden by Herrera), Mottet and Fuerte to their own devices

If the landscape could dwarf the Tour, it would be here at the glacier of la Meije. Tour de France, 1987

Tour de France: *l'Alpe d'Huez*

The most striking thing about the Tour de France is its sheer size – inconceivable, smothering anything and everything in its path, as well as hogging the attention of all of mainland Europe for the whole of July. The Tour also takes over the minds and bodies of the people working on the race: press, radio and TV people and their accompanying technicians as well as the riders and organisers. For three weeks or more their only interest will be the Tour. But there is one place where the Tour meets its Goliath: in the Pyrenees, but more especially in the Alps, the same moving spectacle that can paralyse a big city is itself dwarfed by the powerful physical presence of the mountains.

For the photographer the mountains are the essence of the Tour. There, in the Savoie and Dauphiné Alps, it's no longer a case of cyclist versus cyclist, but of man versus nature. It was the old bromide prints, taken in the glorious days of cycling when riders sometimes had to carry their bikes over the mountains, in *Miroir-Sprint* magazine that inspired so many of us modern-day cycling photographers. And with each passing day in the mountains we all know, feel, that we in our turn are part of the same history-making process: who knows how many young people will be inspired by the images we are capturing now?

Each year as the Tour enters the mountains the link with the past is strengthened. As we climb the Col du Tourmalet in the Pyrenees, or the Col du Galibier in the Alps, I think not only of what I'm seeing now but of incidents from years past. So in 1988 on l'Alpe d'Huez, watching the battle for supremacy between Pedro Delgado and Steven Rooks stirred memories of a decade of photographing this famous climb; the speed of Michel Pollentier in 1978 as he rode away from Hinault and Zoetemelk into the yellow jersey, only to be thrown out of the race for a drug infringement; the power of Laurent Fignon as he rode to his first Tour title in 1983; the following year when the Alpe hosted perhaps its finest moment – the battle between Colombian Luis Herrera and the two French stars, Fignon and Hinault; in 1986, Hinault's symbolic pacing of Greg LeMond all the way up the Alpe after the pair had ridden away from the field two hours earlier. As they crossed the finish line they held each other's arms aloft. But our 1988 story begins on the Col de la Madeleine, where at nearly 2000 metres the peloton is disintegrating under the stress of such a long, steep climb. Beyond this most beautiful of climbs lies the fearsome Col du Glandon and beyond that – at the end of a six and a half hour day – l'Alpe d'Huez.

There's a crystalline quality to the light at this altitude: the clear rays of the sun, intensified by the glaciers high above us, cast an almost fluorescent light onto the riders' glistening faces. My driver Jan and I are driving in the middle of a small group of riders many minutes behind the leaders, and I'm studying the face of Sean Kelly close-up through a 180 mm lens. Staring at Kelly's agonised face from a distance of less than ten feet is an unnerving experience: it's a shock to see this great man suffer. The longer I focus on Kelly the more self-conscious I feel, free to nip in and out on the motorbike recording this image of pain. Even though we're right in amongst the riders none of them complains despite what they must be enduring, but then I realise that these men are barely aware of us, their minds lost to everything but beating the mountain.

After a few minutes I'm content, and Jan wiggles his bike out of the group. Lured by the la Lauzière peak that towers above the summit of the Col, we speed up to the leaders. The final kilometre is a beauty; I stop on the bend below the summit, seizing the opportunity to photograph Herrera and Parra as they ride side by side, with the snow-mass of the Lauzière towering thousands of feet above. Today's is the first real mountain stage and it's been hard to take all the excitement in my stride, so I

wait here for a few minutes to collect my thoughts. Once the real climbing has begun, the adrenalin that has been building up in my system for more than a week surges out, and I'm thankful for this breathing space. The road below us is dotted with dropped cyclists, including Kelly and two of his faithful team-mates. Soon the climb will be over and they can recover on the descent – until the next mountain.

We begin the 20 km descent into the valley, but before we are a quarter of the way down, and despite averaging 100 kilometres an hour, dropped riders start to catch us up. As a courtesy to Jan I watch out behind, even though his eyes are constantly flicking up and down, between the road ahead and his rear-view mirrors. When the riders get within fifty metres of us they shout a warning and we're obliged to move as close to the left as possible, giving them a clear run down the mountain. Among the disjointed groups passing us, two riders catch my eye: Frederic Vichot and Jaanus Kuum. They are clearly enjoying themselves, duelling with each other, left arms tucked in behind to aid their streamlining. Jan and I stay close to these two daredevils, amused by their indulgence. Then Vichot, an ace descender, lives up to his reputation as a showman by pulling alongside on a gentle left-hand bend and shaking the handlebars of the motorbike! Then, after checking the Honda's speedometer (it showed over ninety kilometres an hour), Vichot winks at us before resuming his tuck position and catching up his companion. But then Kelly catches us all up and I know that means his team car, and its ferocious driver, won't be far behind.

As the road starts to twist and turn the KAS team car arrives right on our tail. Coming down as we are, separated from the other motorbikes, we are more exposed to danger from service car drivers, and this driver – Christian Rumeau – is the most notorious. For the next fourteen kilometres he drives a few feet behind

us, sometimes at more than 100 kilometres an hour, denying my driver the freedom he needs to steer cleanly into each bend. At each hairpin the car behind locks its wheels, each screech of rubber shredding my nerves. I look around at him, his expression impassive, eyes barely discernible behind dark glasses. Rumeau is honestly an amiable fellow normally, and denies he's anything else behind the wheel of a car! I'm thankful to reach the bottom − it's been a tough ride down.

We're now approaching the foot of the Glandon, and a group of thirty-five rides swiftly up the lower slopes, propelled by the Reynolds team-mates of Delgado. The battle begins as the road rises above the tree-line at the hamlet of St Colomban-des-Villards. Still eleven kilometres to the top, yet so steep that a group of about ten sheds all the rest, including the yellow jersey of Steve Bauer. We drop back to film the Canadian as he fights to limit his losses, then make our way back up to the leaders, inching past the team cars encouraging their dropped riders. With less than three kilometres to go the road reaches a deep corner at the foot of les Aiguilles de l'Argentière, the range of peaks which the Glandon pass will breach. I'm standing up behind Jan for some pictures of the unfolding scenery when Delgado takes off from the group just in front of us. Jan spots this move at the same moment as I do, and we immediately shoot round the hesitating riders. In four or five seconds we're up to the fleeing Spaniard, but we're not quick enough − already three other motorbikes, including the French TV bike that's now sending live pictures to the world, are there before us. Over the two kilometres that remain before the Glandon's magnificent summit, photographers battle to get a decent shot of Delgado as he's joined by lanky Dutchman Steven Rooks. But I take up my position on the summit itself, realising the futility of working against so many French drivers. After the pair have passed, I decide to wait for the stragglers, knowing the long descent will allow me to get up to

Delgado and Rooks well before the start of the final climb. The summit is a mass of people, perhaps the biggest I've ever seen there. Several spectators are performing the ritual of handing the riders folded newspapers to push up their jerseys for the chilly descent. I spend fifteen minutes shooting these scenes before deciding it's time to be off. As we drop gently down my mind goes back to 1982, when the Tour last came up the Glandon. Then it had been a scorching hot afternoon and I had sunbathed for three hours waiting for the race to arrive. No time for that today − nor the weather: most spectators are huddled in coats or anoraks against the cold.

The wonderful meandering descent of the Glandon is quite a contrast to the earlier Madeleine. Here, the long, long, straights enable us to make a speedy return to the group chasing Delgado and Rooks and at the same time outstrip any rogue drivers. We thread our way through the confusion of team cars, every *directeur-sportif* trying to get up to his rider to pass on advice on how to tackle the final − and hardest − part of the stage: l'Alpe d'Huez. But not everyone can make it. Paul Koechli, Steve Bauer's *directeur-sportif*, grabs my attention as we pass. 'Tell Steve to stop working!', he demands, indignant that Bauer, having made up a lot of time, is apparently riding flat out at the head of this large group. It's not unusual to be asked to pass on information like this, although strictly speaking it's against the rules. We continue making our way up to and past the twenty riders, strung out in a long line. Sure enough, as we speed past, the yellow jersey of Bauer is on the front. But in the seething mass of cars and motorbikes I decide against passing on Koechli's instructions, reasoning that Bauer would be oblivious to any shouted message, such was the intensity of his efforts, and the noise from the hooting cars and motorbikes.

It takes a minute or so to reach the cluster of vehicles behind Delgado and Rooks. They are pacing each other

The effort of climbing the Col de Glandon shows on the face of Dag-Otto Lauritzen as he breasts the summit

all the way along the valley, but as the road is shaded by trees I decide to go ahead and wait just before Bourg d'Oisans. There's a peculiar silence as we wait for the race on the deserted road. Above and behind us a steep rock face stands out, its grey facade sprinkled with small coloured dots – the hundreds of thousands of people waiting to see the Tour de France. They will be lining every inch of the 14 km climb, two deep in most places but four deep on the twenty-two hairpin bends that will take the heroes of the Tour up to 1860 metres. But the reputation of the Alpe owes more to the severity of its first few *lacets* than its length.

On the first of these straights we tuck in behind Delgado and Rooks. L'Alpe d'Huez is by no means the prettiest of the famous Tour climbs, but as most of it is unshaded it is easy to work on technically – except for the final two kilometres, where the narrowness of the road, combined with the density of the crowd, makes it almost impossible. The sun throws a glaring light on to the riders' backs as they turn into the first of the numbered bends. Then it's familiar territory: a shot from behind as they climb the second *lacet* with the snow-covered Massif des Ecrins on the horizon, then wide-angle shots from the rocks above the fourth and fifth bends. Now for a few minutes I can take a breather: I'm happy with what I've got of the two leaders, so I wait for the next riders. In ones and twos they ride past; Parra and Theunisse, then Hampsten by himself, then Herrera and Alcala, followed immediately by Bauer. I take a close-up with my Bronica on the outside of the bend. I'm pleased to see Bauer still fighting; so is Koechli, who playfully steers his car at me as I crouch in the middle of the road.

Now the Alpe is making itself felt. Less than a third of the way up the leaders are spread all over the mountain, each riding a personal time trial of survival. In some – Hampsten and Herrera – I notice deterioration; in others – Bauer and Thierry Claveyrolat

– a strengthening spirit. But it is the two pairs ahead who are grabbing the media attention. Now above the halfway mark, a minute or so still separates the two sets of riders. I pick off a few close shots of Parra as he churns his way up the climb, ignoring Theunisse sitting happily behind him. Delgado and Rooks, however, are both working; indeed for the most part they ride side by side. Twelve months earlier, when they were in the same team, they had been in a similar position. Then, in an epic race, Delgado had shed Stephen Roche and stormed his way into the yellow jersey, leaving the Irishman to struggle all the way to the top. At the end of this day, too, Delgado would once again wear the yellow jersey: but this year, it would be for good.

Five kilometres from the top things start to get interesting. The bends come at you with increasing rapidity, making it hard to concentrate on what's actually happening as riders continually swop positions. Then there's the altitude, hampering the riders' breathing and this photographer's thinking as the thin air loses its oxygen. But the most exciting thing now is the people: denser, more voluble, more colourful than below, and most significantly, 99 per cent Dutch. Since 1976, when Joop Zoetemelk won the stage, the 'Hollanders' have made l'Alpe d'Huez their own: Dutch riders have always performed well here, two wins by Peter Winnen, one by Hennie Kuiper, and another from Zoetemelk in 1979 justifying this cruel mountain's nickname of 'Little Holland'.

But 1988 could be a vintage year for the Dutch: two of their men, Rooks and Theunisse, are in with a chance of winning the stage – or even the Tour. Jan and I had been driving to and fro between the two pairs, stopping as often as possible to compose shots on each hairpin bend, never noticing how close they were getting. In the last five kilometres, realising theirs was *the* break of the Tour, I busied myself with Delgado and Rooks. Working alternately with a 180 mm lens on my Nikon F3 and close

STEVE BAUER

14 July 1988: l'Alpe d'Huez, France

The gruelling ascent of l'Alpe d'Huez is the last place you'd expect to find a stockily-built former ice-hockey player defending the yellow jersey of the 1988 Tour de France. But defending it Canadian Steve Bauer certainly was. He'd won it first on stage one of the Tour: lost it the same day in a team time trial: won it back six days later in Nancy, and for the last three days had been preparing himself for this stage and this mountain — nobody except himself expected

Bauer to be still wearing yellow at the end of the day. But Bauer is never happier than when the odds are stacked against him; he'll go out and race regardless.

He'd been dropped — and virtually forgotten — on the preceding climb of the Col du Glandon, but a superb piece of descending and a do-or-die chase along the valley leading to 'the Alpe' had put Bauer back in contention. At the foot of the mountain he'd led a group of fifteen onto the dreaded climb, a minute and a half behind the escapers, Delgado and Rooks. I'd seen him again less than halfway up, when all the climbers in the group — Parra, Herrera, Theunisse, Boyer, Hampsten, Pensec, Roux and Winnen — had left him. Even so, apart from these eight noted climbers and the man still keeping pace with him, Thierry Claveyrolat, the 'non-climber' Bauer had left the rest of the field — including the likes of Pino, Arroyo, Alcala and Cubino — behind. I decided to follow Bauer and his shadow for a few kilometres: maybe get few more shots of what looked like being his last day in the yellow jersey.

But I began to doubt the conventional wisdom when, with the worst of the incline behind him, Bauer started to eat up the distance between him and the two Frenchmen, Pensec and Roux. As he passed them, much to their amazement, Bauer realised his late surge could pick off one or two more climbers and he began to ride like a man possessed. The next to succumb was Hampsten, winner of the mountainous Giro d'Italia. The styles of the two North Americans couldn't have been more of a contrast: pencil-slim Hampsten, arms and legs tailor-made for this kind of riding, out of the saddle trying to find some zip, and bulldog-shaped Bauer, calves and thighs like tree-trunks, more a track sprinter than a potential Tour winner, sitting deep on his saddle the whole time, using his equally strong arms and shoulders to drive his body on.

I knew what it meant to him to be wearing the yellow jersey, for I'd been photographing Steve from his first professional race, when he'd taken a brilliant bronze medal in the 1984 world championship race — just after his silver medal in the Los Angeles Olympics. I'd been impressed by him then and many times since, but always the big success had eluded him — until, perhaps now.

And right now, Bauer was fighting back — all the way to the finish in l'Alpe d'Huez. Digging ever deeper into his reserves, he picked off Boyer and Winnen: when he finally wheeled into the finish, he'd failed by just twenty-five seconds to keep his yellow jersey . . .

up with my Bronica and fill-in flash, I used up more than two rolls of film on these two alone. It was perfect: two great cyclists pedalling side by side all the way up l'Alpe d'Huez. Even their styles seemed complementary; the rugged Dutchman riding out of the saddle, pitting the superior leverage of his longer legs against Delgado's masterful climbing style.

Two kilometres to go and just a few bends left. Bend number three has always been my favourite. It's not over-populated, and the distant view of the mountains calls attention to the height. But its real worth to me lies in the uncanny way in which, at this point, all the riders stare up to the top of the mountain as if to say 'How far to go?' My best pictures from the Alpe have all been taken there, and none better than the famous ride, in 1986, of Hinault and LeMond. I reflected on the contrasts between then and now. That year I had had to wait several hours here, knowing I would only get the one chance at a good shot, but thriving on the anxiety. For the past two years I had been with the mighty Tour cavalcade, on the back of a motorbike the whole way, getting more and more disorientated with each bend, never getting quite the shot I'd wanted. Until bend number three, that is.

This time it is Parra and Theunisse who give me my best shot of the Tour, Parra leading the duo, his powerful body thrusting the bike out of the corner, eyes fixed on some invisible object high above. It was a vision, and I felt no need to stay any longer.

As soon as we left we were engulfed in chaos. I knew the two pairs of riders had got dramatically close – I'd barely had time to re-cock the Bronica at the last stop. I could see what the trouble was; one of the official guests' cars was moving slowly just ahead of the race, holding up a veritable army of media motorbikes. The racing was ruined as the cyclists filed slowly past the motorbikes. Within sight of the final kilometre sign Jan managed to get away, past the three riders left together,

Rooks having escaped in the jam. We arrived at the cluster of vehicles around Steven Rooks as photographers fought for a better shot at the flying Dutchman and the French television driver punched a photographer who was getting too close. Hardly surprising that the Tour organisers called a meeting that night to censure us all.

But one man could not have cared less about our problems. Despite a brilliant counter-attack by Steve Bauer, Delgado was the new race leader, and for the riders the Alpe was over for another year. Though the mountains were far from finished, in this particular Tour none would be so absorbing as l'Alpe d'Huez.

Is there life after the Tour?

Three full months of the season are left when the Tour de France finally comes to a halt on the Champs Elysées in late July. Yet such is the magnitude of this event that it is hard to see the rest of the season as anything more than an anti-climax, winding down gradually to the final road race of the year, the Tour of Lombardy.

But the racing still holds interest, with the world championships, the Grand Prix des Nations time trial, the Nissan Classic, Paris-Tours and . . . Lombardy. Preparing the riders for these events are the short national Tours of Denmark, Belgium and Holland and the precocious Tour of Britain – events designed to inject fresh stamina into the riders after a fortnight of two-hour criteriums, or 'appearance' races. Some of us are so addicted to the sport that we can't wait for the world championships at the end of August, and a visit to one of these criteriums is the only way to satisfy our

CLAUDE CRIQUIELION

28 AUGUST 1988: RONSE, BELGIUM

The finish straight for the world road-race championship was long, on a stiff rise, and gave us a good view from where we stood behind the finish line. 700 metres away three riders appeared like tiny ants, jigging from side to side across the width of the road. One of them – Steve Bauer, Maurizio Fondriest or Claude Criquielion – would be the new professional champion of the world.

Engulfed by official cars in front and a horde of motorbikes behind, the trio slowly worked its way towards us. Through my 300 mm lens I could see all the switching going on, and Bauer appeared to be the most active. At 150 metres to go he was on the left; at 120 metres, back on the right. The ants had at last grown to an acceptable size in my viewfinder, and through my Nikon I saw Bauer reach for his gear-lever in a last-ditch attempt to recapture the speed he had been losing with every metre of the rise. Fondriest was lagging behind, apparently too much in awe of the struggle in front of him to offer any challenge. Criquielion made his move; injudiciously, to the right of Bauer and into the narrowest of gaps. Then it happened: a distinct collision between the Canadian and the Belgian. Bauer stalled, and Criquielion hit the ground, sending the photographers into a frenzy of clicking shutters. Fondriest, scarcely able to believe his luck, crossed the line first.

The crowd went beserk, screaming abuse at Bauer – and Fondriest – even before the Italian had crossed the line. The photographers went mad too, breaking through the barriers and sprinting down the road: no time now for finer feelings for the forlorn figure limping up the road, one arm raised in a pitiful protest.

'Crikky' is one of the most photogenic men in the peloton. His well-proportioned body, swarthy complexion and bushy eyebrows constantly draw our attention. And he is popular too; never heard to be anything but polite, never seen to be anything but graceful. His glorious athleticism is a joy to see. Criquielion, who won the Worlds in 1984, was for me the worthiest wearer of the rainbow jersey since Hinault won it in 1980. Which made the dramatic events in Ronse all the more poignant: had it not been for the collision, I believe Criquielion would have won.

Triumph — the ecstasy came a moment later. Stephen Roche
crosses the line at Villach, 1987

craving. But the season-long merry-go-round doesn't resume in earnest until the first weekend of September and the World Professional Road Race Championship.

The world championship is a nation-by-nation competition, and it's strange trying to pick out familiar faces wearing national, not trade, jerseys. It is also a different type of photographic challenge: it is the first of only two occasions when we work without a motorbike, and the emphasis is thankfully placed on the photographer's skills rather than those of his driver. The ultimate test is taking the best finish picture, for we know that – as with the Poggio in Milan-San Remo – our editors will splash the finish across two pages, or even the cover.

The world champion gets to wear a special jersey in every race he rides. The *arc-en-ciel,* or 'rainbow' jersey, is the most attractive of all the jerseys and the wearer of it can expect to be the most photographed cyclist in the next twelve months, with the rainbow-coloured hoops standing out from the biggest peloton like a beacon. So one priority in the remaining events of the season is to capture a stock of pictures of the new champion as the racing heads for its winter hibernation.

Since the world champion is usually unwilling to submit his newly-acquired status to public scrutiny quite so soon, the Grand Prix des Nations – the next major event in the calendar – often has to make do without him. Set in the idyllic region around Cannes in the south of France, this 90 km time trial is a particularly attractive assignment, especially because, once again, we are exercising our skills in the absence of motorbikes: by judicious use of a car and map it is possible to photograph each competitor four times during the course of a twice-lapped circuit. But the speed with which the sun sets after the race, casting shadows over the sun-worshippers still supine on the white sand, is a rueful reminder that autumn is imminent . . .

A study in intensity. A fresh-faced Greg LeMond on his way to his first Tour stage, Lac de Vassivière, near Limoges, 1985 (opposite), and (above) on the Col d'Eze, Paris-Nice, 1986

GREG LeMOND

21 APRIL 1987: CALIFORNIA

When you are woken up at two o'clock in the morning by the telephone ringing it's only natural to expect the worst. So as I stumbled downstairs to answer it I was expecting to hear the voice of a friend or relative in trouble. Instead, it was the public relations manager of the Look-Toshiba team calling from Paris. 'Greg's been shot', she blurted out.

'What?' I replied, scarcely able in my half-asleep state to believe what I'd heard: 'Greg shot – is he dead?' Three minutes later, having given her the telephone number she hoped would produce more information, I trudged slowly back to bed, completely dazed by this terrible news.

It must have been the same everywhere as journalists heard about the hunting accident that had left Greg LeMond almost dead from loss of blood, and then rang other journalists to seek more information; their minds full, as mine was, of suddenly poignant memories . . . his second place in the 1982 Goodwood Worlds; his dream win a year later in Switzerland; his first Tour de France stage win in 1985 – so refreshing, coming when Hinault's fifth Tour win was imminent. And of course, there was his glorious victory over Hinault in 1986: that was a moment to savour! I particularly remembered his symbolic ride side by side with Hinault on l'Alpe d'Huez, and his youthful grin as he stepped up to the podium a week later in Paris . . .

Fortunately for LeMond – and cycling – he recovered from his injuries, and actually returned to racing later that year. Fortunately, because his importance to the sport goes a long way beyond his victories and the effect that his rumoured salaries and appearance fees have had on cycle racing which, before his arrival on the scene, allowed its stars to be amongst the worse recompensed of any sport. His biggest influence has been on the growth of the sport in North America where his own successes, and those of the American team in the Los Angeles Olympics, have given new life to cycling in general and cycle racing in particular. And in 1983, when Sean Kelly had yet to win his first classic and a major victory was still eluding Phil Anderson, Greg LeMond put new heart into us English-speaking fans of the sport with his victory in the Worlds.

The photographers like LeMond for a number of reasons; he's eternally fresh-faced, polite to a degree, has a genuinely big smile – and his presence at the head of a breakaway is certain to produce excitement, and therefore good racing. Physically, he is an almost perfect cyclist: neat, compact body; well-defined calves, not over-large but muscular thighs – the epitome of every boy racer's aspirations. The only black mark against him from our point of view is those sun-shades; together with his friend Phil Anderson, LeMond started a craze amongst cyclists that is the curse of photographers everywhere: when a cyclist's eyes can express so much, not to be able to see them . . .

The warm glow of mellow sunlight is an essential ingredient of the atmosphere of the Grand Prix des Nations. Here Charly Mottet tops the Côte de Vallauris on the way to his first 'Nations' victory in 1985

Nissan International Classic

In 1985 a new race swept onto the world stage, injecting some much needed excitement into a season all but played out. The Nissan International Classic Tour of Ireland was launched on the tidal wave of support for Sean Kelly and his younger compatriot Stephen Roche, and immediately became one of the most popular races in the world. Its attraction for a photographer, especially this late in the season when one's inspiration needs constant coaxing, is considerable. The immeasurable beauty of the country and the warmth of its people combine with some exhilarating crowd scenes to fix the race permanently in my memory. One place in particular – St Patrick's Hill in Cork – has a special place in my affections. Its 25% slopes did for the Nissan what the Koppenberg did for the Tour of Flanders: created drama. Each year the hill has left some lasting impression: the deafening crescendo of noise through which Stephen Roche rode to a stage victory in 1985; the fall of Kelly the following year when the modern-day patron saint fluffed a gear change . . . Now the hill is considered unsafe and has gone the way of the Koppenberg.

The racing returns to mainland Europe a week later for the penultimate one-day classic, Paris-Tours. It used to be one of the most famous, but with the season so long and tiring, it now acts merely as a benefit for the sprinters and training for the few remaining cyclists in with a chance of winning the last great race of the year in Italy, a week later.

Giro di Lombardia

There can be few visual images that compare with the tranquillity of Italy's Lake Como under the glow of a warm, mid-October sun. And for a photographer there can be no better way to close the season than with the Lombardia – some might even say the race was planned with a photographer in mind, with its mixture of harsh ascents, leaf-strewn lanes, wonderful lakeside panoramas and – most of all – mellow, seductive autumnal light.

As if realising this aesthetic appeal, the organisers kindly take the route around the western shores of Lake Como in the first few hours. Here, before the serious commencement of hostilities in the peloton, the more sentimental amongst us can direct our gaze away from the race and into the ice-blue waters of the lake, allowing the reflections to take us back over the season's adventures. Until recently the race ran the opposite way, skirting this side of the lake in the final approach to Como; then the enchanting waters of the lake blended with the rich late-afternoon sun to illuminate epic battles between Moser, Hinault, Saronni and Kelly, their faces glowing with concentration.

It is with a strong nostalgia for the passing of the season that the photographer travels to Lombardy. There in Como, with a few minutes to go before the race begins, it is time for goodbyes. Friendships that began at some long forgotten training race and grew – or not – over the season, now come back into focus. For the first time in nine months the members of the peloton want to talk to you as more than just members of the press; to ask if your own season has been a success or failure, and to wish you a restful winter. Seven hours later, when the race arrives on the Corsa Buenos Aires in Milan, it's all over, and we say goodbye until the following year . . . sadness, happiness, fatigue, relief – all these feelings compete for attention. All that's left is the journey home to a quiet winter: but when's that first cyclo-cross? And that big six-day? . . .

St Patrick's Hill, Cork: Sean Kelly's fall in front of his home crowd.
A few seconds later all four of his faithful team-mates dropped
their bikes and rushed to his aid, bringing the race — and the
hearts of the crowd — to a stop!

Stephen Roche playing to the gallery. The man behind the mask is the long-suffering Paul Kimmage

STEPHEN ROCHE

4 SEPTEMBER 1987: VILLACH, AUSTRIA

The photographers were poised for action, more than sixty of us spread out on either side of the long, rising straight. The finish of the world championship was about to take place, and nervous strain was etched into every face as we checked and re-checked our focus on the white line twenty metres away.

Who would win? A large group had started the last lap together – surely a sprinter, maybe Argentin or Kelly . . . The cyclists rode into view from under the road bridge 400 metres down the straight. Gazing through my 300 mm lens, the unmistakable figure of Stephen Roche, dangling off the front of a large group, set my heart pounding. No, it wasn't possible – he couldn't win this one, too – not after the season he'd been having. He reminded me of a third category amateur trying for his first win – head down, sprinting out of the saddle, elbows poking out, skinny legs desperately pushing him on. This frantic apparition came closer; now it was time to change to my 180 mm lens, but still I didn't believe he'd do it – wouldn't believe it, not

until I knew for sure. Then it was all over; gone was the novice-like figure whose wild sprint seemed to have gone on so long, and the cyclist in the green jersey suddenly straightened up, threw his arms in the air and smiled the conscious smile of one who's just made history.

This image of Roche is immortal to me, crowning as it did a season crowded with other images: a forlorn chase in Paris-Nice after Roche's puncture had given Kelly the race on a plate; spectators spitting at him on the Marmolada climb in the Giro d'Italia after he deposed Visentini as race leader; hauling himself up l'Alpe d'Huez in an effort to save his yellow jersey from Delgado, and riding himself to collapse at la Plagne next day – again, to stave off Delgado. Cyclists are by definition a courageous breed, but there is none braver than Roche. He is the tiger in the peloton, snarling his way through the races and clawing at anyone who gets between him and winning. For Stephen Roche doesn't race to come second – not ever.

The Irishman is also a friend to photographers. Add to his combative nature an indefatigable sense of fun and you have the very thing to entertain us when the racing is quiet. Because he's so vulnerable to illness and injury it's hard to place his standing exactly, but I'm sure if Tom Simpson were around today he would regard Stephen Roche as his ideal successor.

An uncaged tiger: Stephen Roche in the Giro d'Italia, 1987

Still bearing the scars of his crash at St Etienne in 1985, Hinault struggles to limit his losses at Luz Ardiden

BERNARD HINAULT

13 OCTOBER 1984: COMO, ITALY

The eyes staring back at me through my 135 mm lens were penetrating, so penetrating that I wanted to look away, just at the moment when I most needed to concentrate on focusing. The eyes belonged to Bernard Hinault, and the urgency was because the great French champion had just made his winning escape in the closing stages of the 1984 Giro di Lombardia. I'd been alongside Hinault a few kilometres earlier as he'd chased a two-man break along the shore of Lake Como, but then there had been other

distractions, like Hinault's rock-solid pedalling rhythm, and the smooth rolling of his shoulders in tune with the pumping motion of his powerful legs. Now, halfway up the San Fermo della Battaglia climb, all I could see was his glaring eyes and expressive Gallic face. And what a face: jaw set stiff in obstinacy (or arrogance?), lips drawn back tightly over clenched teeth, bushy, sun-bleached eyebrows that on any other face would have subjugated the small brown eyes – but not Hinault's . . . Those eyes, that used to paralyse his rivals' ambition, have almost inspired an industry in themselves, appearing on the covers of cycling magazines all over the world and, in France, on the cover of *Paris-Match* and other society journals.

In all my photography of Hinault, starting with his first Tour de France win in 1978, I never failed to be impressed with the way he rode into view – always at the front of a group climbing in the mountains, or driving along a breakaway in the one-day classics. Wherever I pointed my camera, it seemed Hinault was always centre-stage, the dominant figure in every situation. There have been many highlights in his career, but two in particular appealed to me: the 1980 World Championship in Sallanches, when just two months after abandoning the Tour de France with a serious knee injury, Hinault rode lap after lap on the front before finally taking off with the Italian Baronchelli for company – and of course going on to win the world title; and the 1985 Tour de France, when Hinault suffered a terrible crash in a big sprint in St Etienne, halfway through the Tour, emerging next day with his broken face to fight on – and eventually win his fifth Tour. He was the stuff legends were made of – and he knew it.

Even now he has retired from racing I find myself drawn to his dark head as he leans through the sun-roof of his official Tour car; the eyes hidden by sun-glasses, but his pouting lips betraying his thoughts. His aloof presence still manifests the power he used to exert over the peloton, and the racing is taking time to adjust to his absence. Occasionally, when he barks a reprimand at one of us photographers for being in the way, it's easy to understand why many of his rivals were simply too scared to challenge his authority!

For like him or not, it has to be said that Hinault has class – and in racing knew exactly when and how to use it. Despite his faults, his arrogance and obstinacy, he still remains for me the most mysterious and enigmatic of them all.

CRASH!

20 APRIL 1988: GHENT-WEVELGEM

Cyclists sprawled on the ground, confirming those tell-tale signs that precede such incidents: a violent swerve amid the speeding bunch, a squeal of brakes, sometimes a shout. Then you see them – cyclists piling on top of one another. Without hesitation my driver René turns up the throttle and, almost before I've had time to react, we brake to a halt behind the stricken victims.

But we're not alone, for on both sides of us BMW and Kawasaki motorbikes carry to the scene their cargo of photographers, primed like me to react quickly to such an event. No time is lost as we jump off our bikes and scatter amongst and around the fallen cyclists. Unusually, the photographers have got there first – more often than not the mechanics and team managers beat us to it – so there's ample opportunity for us to get our precious pictures before the moment is lost. I have a split second after a crash to make my choice; then I am committed and have to stick with it whatever the other photographers are doing. I make a beeline for the instantly recognisable Z Peugeot rider Gilbert Duclos-Lassalle, while even as I'm shooting I can see out of the corner of my eye that most of the others are crowded around a Carrera rider who seems to be in need of medical attention. But I am convinced that I've made the 'better' choice, and fire away through a 35 mm lens.

I sensed it was time to catch up with the rapidly moving bunch and we sped off, but the sense of shame I had felt since the previous Sunday's Liège-Bastogne-Liège strengthened its hold. 'What am I doing this for?', I had asked myself then, having witnessed and photographed Davis Phinney having a particularly horrid crash.

Over the years I've been covering big races I thought I had become hardened to incidents like this, yet this gloom wouldn't lift. It was almost as if this crash in Ghent-Wevelgem had been one too many, yet I could recall my one-time relish at the possibility of filling my portfolio with pictures of crashes. People often used to tease me about what I'd do if someone I knew crashed badly in a race. 'Would you', they'd ask, 'help him or take pictures first?' Until Liège-Bastogne-Liège this question had remained unanswered; there were always people on hand better qualified than I to help crash victims. All the same, I had quietly believed that if it ever happened my immediate concern would be for the welfare of the victim and not for my photography – until Liège-Bastogne-Liège . . .

That day we'd been working our way up through the convoy of team cars delayed by a pile-up involving fifty or sixty riders. I spotted a 7-Eleven jersey nipping between the cars in an effort to get back on. I was amused by the contrast between the rider's torn shorts and immaculate jersey, and instructed my driver to tuck in behind in order that I might get a few shots. It was a decision I was to regret, for as I worked away at what I thought would be a 'light relief' picture, I realised that something was wrong – Phinney hadn't seen the stationary service car just twenty metres in front of him. In that instant I took the camera away from my eye as if I couldn't believe what was about to happen. I shouted – as did René – yet it was so late that it was more like a scream: we watched the American smash face first through the rear window of the car.

My reaction was instant, as if the previous five seconds had been a slow dream. Without thinking I re-aimed with my Nikon, aware of another photographer already shooting away next to me. In ten seconds I knocked off nearly twenty shots using two cameras before my conscious mind caught up: this time there was nobody there to help – no 'qualified' person. 'What the hell am I doing,' I thought, 'I know this poor guy.' In the few minutes it took for help to arrive – fortunately the 7-Eleven team car was approaching – I did my best to comfort an all-too-conscious Phinney, yet I left the

Davis Phinney's crash in Liège-Bastogne-Liège, 1988

Shooting brutal images like this is a heart-rending job; fortunately, after this crash in the 1983 Amstel Gold, Twan Poels was racing again in less than three weeks

scene sickened by my actions and at having finally found the answer to that question.

From the first time I ever photographed a road race crash – in the 1982 Paris-Nice – I have never ceased to be amazed at the tolerance extended to photographers, especially when they appear to be getting in everybody's way. When a big stack-up happens, it's complete chaos. Everything immediately behind the race stops instantly, car doors fly open as mechanics rush out with spare wheels, race officials try to clear a path for the convoy to get through. And all around and amongst this, photographers are at work.

As soon as you see, or more likely hear, a crash, you shout at your driver to stop (he probably hasn't heard the crash as he's wearing a normal crash helmet. Photographers tend to adopt a variety of doubtful-looking helmets, not to snub safety but so that they can hear properly and hold a camera freely up to their faces.) Having stopped, preferably as close to the source of the crash as possible, you leap off, dodging among the other motorbikes that litter the road. Then it's a question of experience; seek out instantly what's most important to you, as they won't be on the ground for long. Maybe an English-speaking rider? Or equally 'good', a Fignon or a Van der Poel? Sometimes, if you arrive late at the scene of a crash, you can judge its importance immediately by the number of photographers; some of the more experienced cameramen might not even bother stopping for lesser-known victims! It only happens rarely, but when one of the really top riders is caught in a crash there is pandemonium – as Kelly's crash in the 1987 Tour de France demonstrated.

Some of the best pictures are to be had immediately after a crash as a rider chases to get back on. If a star rider has been delayed, the chances are he'll have his whole team surrounding him. It makes for a spectacular sight.

In any race, a photographer's knowledge of the race's

1987 Tour de France. Kelly has crashed, and photographers swarm around as his team encourages him back to the bunch. I needed to work very close with a wide-angle lens because the area was congested by so many motorbikes

Kelly has climbed off. Photographing him crying in Christian Rumeau's arms left me at least feeling very conscience-stricken . . .

. . . and a few seconds later ashamed to be intruding

characteristics are invaluable. He needs to know exactly where he is at any given moment in order to anticipate incidents. In Milan-San Remo, for example, all the action is packed into the last twenty-five kilometres, and it's usually disastrous to be anywhere but in front of the race at this point, with the short climbs of the Cipressa and Poggio looming up. In 1988, though, a group of three riders broke clear on the Cipressa, and two of us duly followed them over the top. Knowing that the bunch was less than 15 seconds behind, I'd instructed Patrice, my crack French driver, to overtake on the descent before the bunch got to us. But Bruno Cornillet changed those plans . . . the little French cyclist had been leading the trio down the steep, twisting descent, when he overshot a difficult right-hand bend. He slid away into the bushes and his two companions slid after him – they'd been relying on Cornillet to guide them down. I just caught a glimpse of Thierry Marie hitting the deck and then disappearing over the edge of the road beneath a crash barrier. At this stage there were just two of us on motorbikes. Both drivers slammed on the brakes to let us take a very quick shot, but the other photographer decided not to risk it – the bunch was catching us up too fast. We were so close to the Poggio that it was risking seven hours' work for one picture, but something told me to stay.

No sooner had Patrice got the bike off the road than I knew I'd hit the jackpot. The bunch had already started to sweep past us at seventy kilometres an hour, a few of them glancing at Marie as he clambered back up to the road. He was my target, and I began to run up to him when, to my utter disbelief – it is crazy trying to descend with a speeding bunch – an official's motorbike came round the bend. On seeing Marie at the roadside, he braked to a halt, oblivious of the danger to the descending riders. Sure enough, it happened; rider after rider hit the stationary motorbike on the very apex of this sharp bend. They had nowhere to go, and up to a

dozen riders came to grief in front of me, some of them catapulting over the crash barrier and down the steep bank beyond.

It was a heaven-sent opportunity, and I made the most of it. (Although later, viewing the slides, I was a little disappointed to see that I had concentrated more on the carnage around the motorbike than the catapulted riders – it all happens so quickly that often you are not sure what you've got until the films are developed.) Despite the surge of excitement, though, I realised that we had to get out quickly or we'd never get past a group this size before the start of the Poggio. We accelerated into a large gap in the still-descending bunch, incurring the wrath of several riders, but my adrenalin was pumping and I didn't care. Besides, my driver is one of the best on the Continent: even at this speed Patrice was able to overtake on the descent and we arrived with the leaders five or six kilometres before the Poggio. Given that we'd stopped for nearly five minutes, getting back up to the leaders took luck, 1000 ccs of BMW engine, an expert driver . . . and the experience of five previous Milan-San Remos. Nor is it coincidence that some of the best photographers in the business have graduated from being racing cyclists; one of the major prerequisites is to be able to read the way a race is going and position yourself accordingly.

It is equally important to employ the best driver available, because otherwise it's impossible to make the most of your opportunities. The crucial part played by a good driver was demonstrated to me in Ireland in the 1986 Nissan International Classic. In a country with a lot of dairy farming, it is inevitable that the roads and lanes should be liberally strewn with cow-dung. On a stage to Limerick in the west, near the Cliffs of Moher, the race was descending gently when the road suddenly narrowed to about the width of a driveway. On it were a layer of cow-dung and a television motorbike that shouldn't have been in the middle of the bunch at all.

One cyclist lost his grip on the slippery surface, the motorcyclist had nowhere to go and up to twenty people hit the deck. My driver Gerry Murray had been going to overtake, but with his local knowledge had decided to pull back before the hazard became obvious. Even so, we were still inside the rear of the bunch when the television motorbike went down some distance in front of us. Everybody was hitting their brakes; I can vividly recall Joop Zoetemelk skidding by on our inside as Gerry fought to keep his own skid in a straight line, while all around us riders were hitting the ground. Somehow, though neither Gerry or I could quite believe it, we'd not only stayed upright but had avoided running over the cyclists as they slid in front and to the side of us. That's the only time I've actually been caught in the midst of a pile-up, and people were quick to praise the startling pictures that resulted from it – pictures that are still being used today. Yet I know that it was only the driver's skill that enabled me to come up with such rare shots.

The most surprising thing about photographs of crashes, and of people suffering, is the reaction of the victims themselves. Everybody wants a picture of themselves, it seems, no matter how painful the occasion on which it was taken. A few years ago I photographed a stunned Sean Yates lying in a ditch during Ghent-Wevelgem, and his father, whom I know well, was quick to ask me for a set of pictures for the living room wall. And just a few weeks after Phinney's frightful crash I witnessed a curious instance of the rider's point of view. On a visit to the home of the Norwegian cyclist Dag-Otto Lauritzen I produced a copy of *Cyclisme International* featuring all the 'cobbled classics'. After Dag and his wife had exclaimed in horror at the picture of Phinney colliding with the car, Dag spotted a picture of himself crashing in Paris-Roubaix. 'There's me!', he exclaimed, his eyes wide with delight. 'Look: I'm crashing!'

The disorientated figure sitting in the ditch during the 1983
Ghent-Wevelgem is Sean Yates

TRACKMEN

Held usually in the week prior to the road events, the track racing worlds are an exceedingly attractive proposition for the photographer, the wide variety of events stretching his ingenuity and reflexes almost as much as those of the cyclists themselves. Technically, track events are the most difficult of cycling's many disciplines to photograph well: poor, or artificial, lighting, as the events are usually held in the evening; high racing speeds; and the presence of so many ill-informed officials, combine to limit the scope of even the most skilful and best-equipped photographer!

It is in the in-field, where the officials are at their most numerous, that the best photo opportunities are to be found, but there is so much activity and distraction that only an eagle-eyed photographer spots the best pictures. The more athletic amongst us are at an advantage here, covering the 100 metres of in-field at a spring as the distinctive sound of disintegrating spokes reaches our ears, usually from the opposite end . . .

Six-days

Surely the most under-rated, yet glamorous, aspect of cycle racing, six-day racing gives the gentle art of track racing an extended lease of life into the winter months. From mid-October through to February most of Europe's larger cities play host to these 'circus' races, most spectacularly in West Germany where – in cities like Munich, Stuttgart and Berlin – 14–15,000 spectators cram themselves each night into the tiny purpose-built velodromes. In the course of the winter I try to take in at least two of these events, using as an excuse – if one were needed – the introduction of variety into the editorial coverage. It is also an opportunity to complete my own 'Tour of Europe'; West Germany has no national Tour or classic race, the Grand Prix de Frankfurt being the nearest thing, so a visit to one or two six-days is the final piece of the nomadic jigsaw that was started in Spain almost a year before.

114

Going flat out, as in this shot of the 1982 European Omnium championship in Herning, Denmark, Tony Doyle is one of the most photogenic of subjects

Koichi Nakano: until his retirement, one of my favourite characters on the circuit. Here he is performing his pre-race ritual before a world championship sprint-match

Like Nakano, the Russian sprinter Sergei Kopylov was a great favourite with the crowds, thanks largely to his acrobatic prowess – in and out of the racing

A futuristic bike and aerodynamic skin-suit helps Hans-Henrik Oersted to beat the sea-level world hour record at Bassano del Grappa, 1985

WHAT'S IN A PICTURE?

Photographing cycle racing is an action-packed occupation. Every year, between the beginning of February and mid-October, I will spend at least 136 days on the move – and that doesn't count any domestic events, winter six-days or cyclo-crosses, nor indeed any interviews between races, some of which entail travelling long distances. The total time I spend away from home probably adds up to something more like six months.

For the main continental road events I travel more than 35,000 miles to cover about ninety-three days of racing and take over 20,000 pictures. In a one-day classic I expect to use on average ten rolls of film – more in action-packed events like Milan-San Remo and Paris-Roubaix, less for races like Ghent-Wevelgem and the Amstel Gold. In a stage race like the Vuelta or Giro the rate drops, with the steadier pace of the racing, to about six rolls of film a day. Inevitably, the Tour de France eats up film; each day an average of ten rolls, more in the mountains where a stage can hold as much drama and excitement as a top classic – and often more. Including a provision for post-race interviews and special items like photographing mechanics at work my total for the Tour runs to 250 rolls of film.

It's not hard technically to work from the motorbike. But what is really required is a sound knowledge of the race and the route, a good driver, strong nerves and a strong, supple body, as you are constantly twisting right round to shoot over your shoulder. You also need lightning reflexes to cope with a multitude of incidents and a similarly quick mind to direct your driver – he won't act without instructions. The main problem is road vibration, which means that lenses longer than 135 mm are unsuitable, although a 180 mm can sometimes be used to good effect as long as the road surface is good. Sometimes a 35 mm lens is necessary – when the riders are racing close to the motorbike, or immediately after the race has finished. But the best all-round solution

seems to be to have one camera with an 85 or 50 mm lens, and another, identical, camera fitted with a 105 mm or 135 mm lens. Having two, sometimes three, identical cameras means there's no fumbling with unfamiliar controls when you switch from one camera to another. Travelling on a motorbike is restricting in one way: all your equipment has to be carried with you, not easy with just two small panniers – sometimes, none at all.

If it is a rainy day, chances are that at least one of your cameras will be put out of action – cycle racing is tough on camera equipment, photographed as it is under all weather conditions. Once out there on the motorbike there's no shelter for you and your equipment, and even using a chamois leather to keep your equipment dry can't protect it for long. Cameras and lenses need to be serviced three times over a season: once before the start, once after the classics of Flanders and Paris-Roubaix and once after the Tour de France. Every year at least one camera will need replacing.

Although *Visions of Cycling* is full of tales involving motorbikes, my best pictures nearly always come from stationary situations – at the finish line, looking down on the race from a small hill or other vantage point, or simply standing by the side of the road. The real advantage of using a motorbike is that it gives me mobility in and around the race, so I have access to the very best the race and the route has to offer. With the exception of the crash pictures, the best shots are those composed at places along the route, when I have the time to think clearly. On the back of the motorbike you are surrounded by noise and distraction, and the racing dictates what you shoot: considerations like landscape and special effects have to take second place to what's happening in front of you. Less than a quarter of the pictures in this book were taken from the back of a motorbike.

Away from the motorbike, my preferred lens is the 300 mm; sometimes I even carry this bulky, heavy object on the motorbike, as it's great for taking dramatic head-on shots, and for creating interesting landscapes too. I also like a 180 mm for head-on shots where space is too restricted to use the 300 mm; one of the problems of cycle racing is that a group of cyclists always has cars or motorbikes hovering just ahead of them, which makes it difficult to get a clear shot.

An unusual opportunity arose in the 1987 Kellogg's Tour of Britain, when a strong headwind slowed the 180-mile stage from Newcastle upon Tyne to Manchester. As a result the shot on pages 118-119 of the leading break climbing Saddleworth Moor was taken in late-evening sunlight, and this light – and a 300 mm lens – produces the curious illusion that the bicycles are levitating as they crest the summit.

Shooting the finish

Shooting a race finish is an art in itself. There are so many aspects to consider. A single rider, winning alone, is the easiest, as once the lens is chosen (a longer lens is better here as it makes it easier to isolate the rider from the background) all you have to watch out for is the winner lowering his arms before he reaches the finish line!

In a sprint finish, the difficulties multiply. A canny racing mind is a great asset here, as you must calculate which side of the road the winner is likely to take – a decision usually determined by the wind direction or the way the road approaches the line. Having done that, you must be ready for a last-second change of camera or lens if the selected one turns out to be too long or too short. In Continental races, you can rarely use lenses much longer than 180 mm or 200 mm as there is too great a risk of getting other photographers' arms and elbows in the picture. In a big classic or a stage of the Tour de France the lead car is often driven just 50-60 metres ahead of the speeding bunch – sometimes necessary to

clear a path for the riders through the funnel of media people striving for a view of the finish, but a nuisance for photographers wanting a clear view of the run-in. In the picture on page 121 of Van Poppel winning a Tour stage I needed a moderately short 105 mm lens to capture the complete battle – a speeding bunch can take up a wide area of road – and to allow space in the frame for the winner to throw his arms up.

Experience is essential here: a bunch of cyclists speeding towards you at up to 45 miles an hour can be scary. Stay in the road too long and you may be knocked down and even killed – a French photographer has actually died this way. Note the angle at which Van Poppel and his colleagues are veering across the road – to avoid the twenty-odd photographers lined up at an angle to the barriers. Don't worry – a split second after pressing the shutter I too am veering away – to the safety of a metal fence!

NB – Despite popular belief, pictures that show beaten riders apparently using their brakes to slow down are not 'letting' someone else win: the area around the finish is always congested, and they are simply anticipating having to skid to a halt within 50 metres of the finish line.

Fill-in flash

I work a lot with fill-in flash. This technique was first adopted by press agency photographers in the mid-1960s, and since then has been employed by Italians in particular. Nowadays, almost everybody uses it. The attraction is obvious: flash lights up the shadows that a cyclist's hunched-over body creates under a high sun; so, too, flash accentuates the perspiration and strain on the riders' faces. For this technique I use a Bronica 6×4.5 cm camera which allows me to synchronise the flash at 1/500th of a second – a valuable advantage over cameras that operate their synchronisation at a

maximum of 1/250th, which can leave a 'ghost' around the subject – unless, of course, that is what you want. The shot on page 122 of Robert Millar in the 1985 Tour de France prologue is a fair example of fill-in flash, although without any strong sunshine to counter it the flash has dominated the picture, exposing the foreground only.

Portraits

Cyclists are a photogenic breed, their muscular, bronzed bodies complemented by handsome faces. Capturing their expressions is a particular addiction for me, as if the perfect portrait will reveal the chosen subject's true philosophy . . .

There are no rules about shooting portraits; having taken lighting and background into consideration only instinct can tell you whether the picture is going to work. Any lens can be used; on page 123 the unusual portrait of Davis Phinney, shot with a 300 mm lens, shows him in a pensive mood the morning after the last mountain stage of the 1988 Tour. For once the Oakleys enhance the picture!

Landscapes

As with portraits, there are no hard and fast rules to taking good landscape photographs – once again, it is what looks right. Nearly always it is a matter of suiting the lens to the type of shot you want, with the size of the bunch of cyclists the most important factor – especially if the landscape is mountainous. A full peloton usually works best, as the large numbers help balance the visual domination of the mountains: towering peaks can make a small group of cyclists look insignificant.

A long (180 mm or 300 mm) lens can distort the perspective, whereas a moderately wide-angle 24-35 mm lens represents near enough what your eye actually sees. If you're working high up, in the Alps or Pyrenees for example, you must take into account the reflective quality of the snow and adjust the exposure accordingly. The camera's built-in meter will not give you the right result, under-exposing in the bright light. Better to use a hand-held meter with an incidental-light facility and take a reading from the sun itself.

Few landscape shots can compare with a line of cyclists against a backdrop of majestic mountains. For the shot of the Nissan Classic in Ireland which ends the book, I climbed a hill a few hundred feet above the road and used a 28 mm lens to position the mountains and cyclists so that they balance each other in the frame: a high vantage point adds to the impact.

Film stock

Over a season that lasts virtually twelve months, a variety of film stock will be needed to allow for all the changes in lighting conditions, from 'fast' films like 400 ASA in the early spring and late summer events to 100 or even 50 ASA for races in the height of summer. Various parts of Europe at various times of year have their own particular light-quality, and each of these needs special treatment. I try to avoid changing the ASA rating of films as far as possible, to avoid colour changes and 'grain' on the finished slide. However, there are times, especially in early March and at cyclo-cross events on gloomy winter days, that a 400 ASA film will need to be pushed to as much as 1600 or even 3200 ASA.

At other times, particularly when shooting in colour, it is well worth working at the very limit that your equipment offers – 1/500th of a second at full aperture – to retain the clarity of colour transparency film. Except for 'panning' effects I never work at less than 1/500th of a second: a cyclist moves too fast through the line of focus and is himself moving a lot on the bike.

The shot on Saddleworth Moor in the Kellogg's Tour is a good example of using the very last of the available light. Knowing that using a 400 ASA film would have destroyed the quality of the evening sun, I shot it on Fujichrome Professional rated at 100 ASA on a lens that opened as wide as f2.8. Fujichrome has been my favourite film stock for the past four years because of its marvellous colour density and sharpness.

The 1988 Nissan Classic winding its way along the valleys of Connemara